Suppressed Voices

Dr. Ruhail Choudhury

Qurate
qaratebooks.com

SUPPRESSED VOICES
Dr. Ruhail Choudhury

Published in 2025

© Published by

qurate
quratebooks.com

Qurate Books Pvt. Ltd.
Goa 403523, India
www.quratebooks.com
Tel: 1800-210-6527, Email: info@quratebooks.com

ISBN: 978-93-58988-44-4

DISCLAIMER

The views, thoughts and opinions expressed in this book are solely those of the author and are intended to present personal reflections, ideas and concerns based on information available in the public domain or from reliable news sources at the time of writing. While effort has been made to ensure accuracy and credibility, the content should not be considered as verified news, historical record or factual documentation. In the event of any ambiguity, inconsistency or deviation, readers are encouraged to consider the content with critical thinking and interpret it in light of their own understanding and judgement.

This book does not intend to influence beliefs, promote specific ideologies or demand agreement from its readers. Instead, it serves as a medium for open ideas, introspection and the exchange of thoughts. The author does not claim authority over all the subjects discussed, nor does the book aim to establish any definitive stance on sensitive or evolving matters. Any resemblance to real events or individuals is purely coincidental unless explicitly stated. Readers are advised to conduct their own research and consult appropriate experts, if they seek factual clarity on specific topics mentioned herein. This book is shared in good faith and for introspection and reading purposes only.

TRIBUTE TO:

Bhagat Singh

For Supreme Sacrifice

Swami Vivekananda

For Spiritual Awakening

Mahatma Gandhi

For promoting Non-Violence

Bhim Rao Ambedkar

For Social Justice

TRIBUTE TO:

APJ Abdul Kalam

For his Simplicity

Sir Ratan Tata

For Kindness

Justice Bhushan Ramkrishna Gavai

For Humbleness

Vijay Shekhar Sharma

For Innovative Revolution

SOURCES OF INSPIRATION

Nelson Mandela

Mother Teresa

Rabidranath Tagore

Dalai Lama

Martin Luther King (Jr)

Khalil Gibran

Desmond Tutu

Antonio Guterres

Michelle Obama

Greta Thunberg

ALSO INSPIRED BY:

Ruskin Bond

N Ram - The Hindu Group

Dr. Shashi Tharoor

Rajdeep Sardesai

Barkha Dutt

Chetan Bhagat

Shobha De

Special Thanks To:

My Parents, Wife, Daughter and all family members.

Mentors, Teachers and seniors in profession

All Friends, well-wishers and colleagues.

Calcutta High Court Bar Association - Authorities & all members.

Calcutta Club - Authorities & all members.

Eastern Metropolitan Club, kolkata - Authorities & all members.

Harvard University - Dr. Jaauline Bhabha & Team.

Thames International University, Paris & all associates.

The Assembly of God Church School - Teachers & Students.

South Calcutta Law College - Professors & Students.

One 97 Communications Ltd - Paytm:

Mr. Vijay Shekhar Sharma
Mr. Vikrant Bangia
Mr. Avijit Jain
Ms. Urvashi Sahai
Mr. Inder Raj Gill.
Mr. Mayank Verma
Mr. Syed Nehal Azam
Mr. Jasmeet Singh

Mahindra and Mahindra Financial Services Limited:

Ms. Farida Balsara
Chief Legal Officer

Mr. Sudip Ray
Head Litigations

SMFG India Credit Company Ltd:

Mr. Suman Deb - Head Legal
Mr. Mohit Bharadwaj - HOC

Grihum Housing Finance Ltd:

Mr. Manish Jaiswal - MD & CEO

Mr. Amit Kumar Khan - Chief Business Officer.

Eminent Educationist:
Mr. L.W. Hartnett
Mr. John Bagul
Mr. Kanak Gupta
Ms. Kalyani Patnaik
Prof. Federico Jarasat, Argentina.
Ms. Rupkatha Sarkar

Dr. Pramod Mahajan, Sharjah, UAE.
Ms. Gurmeet Bindra
Ms. Chitkala Kalan
Ms. Joeeta Basu
Ms. Sunita Sen
Ms. Joyeeta Mukherjee
Ms. Jayeeta Ganguly
Ms Radhika Sinha
Ms. Kavita Saraf
Mr. Suvendu Mukhopdhyay

The Voices Online Team
Mr. Malay Mukherjee
Dr. Deborshi Batat
Mr. Tathagata Chowdhury

Mr. Imran Zaki
Dr. Lal Bhatia
Ms. Amrita Ghosal & The Echo of India Team.
Mr. D.D.Burman, New Indian Express group.
Mr Amit Chatterjee, Kolkata Police.

Adv Majid Menon
Adv. Pinaki Addy
Adv Anoop Bose
Adv Zafar Iqbal
Adv Paritosh Sinha
Adv Prince Pawaiya
Adv Onkar Gujar
Adv Salim Rahman
Adv Kaushik Chatterjee
Adv Satyaraj - Chennai
Adv Milindo Paul
Adv Sudipto Ganguly, Barasat
Adv Chandrasekhar Sarkar
Adv Ranjit Ghosh
Adv Vineet Sharma
Adv Nafees Khan
Adv Munees Dhawan

FOREWORD

"Suppressed Voices" is an in-depth collection of powerful thoughts about those who are often silenced. Ruhail deeply values freedom of expression for everyone, believing that healing, progress and mutual understanding can only occur when everyone is heard. You'll find the book to be both moving and thought-provoking.

Ruhail is a prolific writer who cares for people's feelings and understands the importance of giving them the freedom to express their voices. Ignoring a voice is a flawed perspective. Nature itself is the best example. Though it watches us, it responds with fury when suppressed and exploited, as seen in many disasters. Ruhail beautifully suggests how suppressed voices can erupt with great intensity when they are not given a platform.

Voices must be heard for society to fully mobilize. We must listen to voices around us, for ourselves, for humanity and for future generations. I hope you find the time to explore these important narratives.

I wanted to share some thoughts on the importance of speaking up and expressing our opinions freely. When we lend our voices to support causes or beliefs we strongly believe in, we empower others who may lack the confidence to speak out. It's about articulating our thoughts in a way that resonates and leaves a lasting impact on those around us.

Great leaders throughout history have shown us that significant change, like achieving Independence through freedom struggles, requires the power of collective voices advocating for a common cause. Similarly, our individual voices gain strength through thoughtful and expressive communication, especially when we speak in one voice.

There's a powerful saying that resonates deeply with me, "The day you do not speak up for the things that matter to you is the day when your freedom truly ends." I firmly believe that expressing our thoughts clearly and openly is essential for personal empowerment and creating a positive environment.

Ruhail's book, "Suppressed Voices," beautifully encapsulates this sentiment. Kudos to his writing and great thoughts.

Mrs. Kalyani Patnaik
Eminent Author & Principal and Head of School
Hiranandani Foundation School & HFS International,
Powai, Mumbai, India.

ABOUT THE BOOK

Suppressed Voices is not merely a book but it is a profound and evocative journey into the dark corners with unheard cries of our society. It is an awakening, an emotional expedition that seeks not to preach but to stir, to move and ultimately, to question the conscience of its readers. Each page is not just written, it is felt, as if the ink itself carries the silent pain of those whose stories remain buried beneath the loudness around us.

In a world flooded with information and constant chatter, there exists a disturbing paradox - the most important voices are often the least heard. These are the voices of the marginalized, the forgotten, the ordinary people who suffer quietly, whose pain is so deeply embedded into the fabric of our everyday life that we no longer pause to notice them. '*Suppressed Voices*' brings these ignored murmurs to the forefront, trying to give them a new voice.

The book does not merely discuss social problems but it compels us to feel them. It confronts issues that are all too familiar like poverty, discrimination, injustice, violence or apathy, it presents them not as statistics or abstract policy failures, but as deeply human experiences, raw and real. The author serves not just as a writer but as a medium, channeling the faint, dying echoes of those who can no longer able to speak for themselves and presenting them with dignity and grace.

There is a quiet philosophy that runs through every chapter, one that reflects the author's core belief - that no voice is truly dead, they are only unheard. Through with each narrative, each thought, the author brings life back into these silenced souls, reminding us that empathy is not a luxury but it is a responsibility. To listen to the unspoken, to care for the unseen and to cry for the unfelt pain of others is what makes us a true human.

In doing so, the book doesn't simply ask the reader to read it but rather invites them to introspect within. To look beyond the surface, to question the familiar, to become uncomfortable with complacency. The hope is not just to inform, but to transform, to kindle a small flame of change in every reader's heart. Because the real power of literature lies not only in beautiful prose, but in its ability to change perceptions, awaken truths and challenge our silence.

Suppressed Voices resonates with a timeless truth - that the strength of a society is measured not by how loud its privileged shout, but by how tenderly it listens to its weakest. The book appeals to our inner conscience, asking - *What kind of society are we building, if so many must suffer unheard?* It gently nudges us to question the comfort of our indifference and dares us to be better, not as critics, but as compassionate human beings.

This is a book that stays with you, not just for its language or insights, but for the emotional imprints it leaves behind. It is not written to impress, but to express - to carry the weight of unspoken grief and to remind us that silence too has a sound and it is often the loudest, yet unheard.

In the end, *Suppressed Voices* is more than a collection of thoughts, it is a quiet revolution. It is a mirror held up to society and perhaps, even more importantly, to ourselves. It is an invitation to listen, to feel, to understand and to act.

Because somewhere, right now, someone's voice is being drowned. And perhaps, after reading this book, we may just be able to hear it.

ABOUT THE AUTHOR

Dr. Ruhail Choudhury is an eminent corporate lawyer, acclaimed writer and socially conscious columnist whose words have left a profound impact on minds and institutions alike. With a deep-rooted passion for justice and human values, he has emerged as one of the most respected voices in contemporary discourse, blending the precision of law with the sensitivity of human understanding.

A law graduate from the prestigious University of Calcutta and further enriched his academic journey with a postgraduate diploma in Personnel Management and advanced certifications in Cyber and Media Law from WBNUJS. Demonstrating a broader commitment to societal issues, he also completed a specialized course in Child Welfare from Harvard University (Harvard X), reflecting his concern for the most vulnerable sections of society.

In recognition of his outstanding contributions to corporate law, Thames International University, Paris, conferred upon him an Honorary Doctorate

(Ph.D.), a testament to his scholarly insight and real-world expertise. His legal career has been marked by sharp intellect, strategic thinking and an unwavering sense of ethics, qualities that have earned him great admiration in the corporate world.

But it is perhaps through his writing that he has reached the hearts and minds of a wider audience. His columns and articles on pressing social issues are regularly featured in leading newspapers and journals, both in India and abroad. Known for their depth, clarity and philosophical resonance, his writings are not mere observations but they are powerful calls for introspection and transformation.

His recent book, "Darkness Unveiled," has received widespread acclaim for its thought-provoking narratives and compassionate insights. The book was honoured with the Golden Book Award and the Ukiyoto Literary Award 2024 at the Kolkata International Literary Carnival, among other accolades such as the TRI Literary Award, further cementing his place among India's emerging and impactful contemporary authors. He also received The Asia Iconic Award from Global Human Rights Council for Peace and Sustainable Development, USA as an acknowledgement for his exemplary efforts to promote international peace though his digital international platform with over 1.5 million viewers across the world, 'The Voices Online' (www.thevoicesonline.com).

What sets him apart is his profound belief that writing is not a profession, but a passion, a medium through which he connects with society at its deepest levels. He said, "There can be no greater satisfaction than knowing that my words are shaping thoughts, stirring emotions and making people reflect on social realities". His writing suggest transforms, compelling readers to engage with the world more compassionately and consciously.

In an era often driven by noise and distraction, Dr. Ruhail Choudhury's voice remains steady, sincere and profoundly human - a rare combination of legal brilliance and literary soul that continues to inspire and enlighten.

PREFACE

The voices of the rich, famous and powerful often reverberate across the globe, expectedly capturing the attention of people all around. There is also a widespread fascination created about their lives, thoughts and activities. In a market-driven world, content that generates high demand tends to be produced in abundance. As a result, it's no surprise that newspapers, magazines, television, radio, websites and all other media outlets are constantly filled with stories about society's most privileged groups and individuals. This media saturation reflects not only public interest but also the business of entertainment and public demand. But what happens to the important yet marginalized voices that often get drowned out in the chaotic noise of loud, glittering and sensational stories? These voices, though significant, are frequently overshadowed by the attention-grabbing narratives of the rich and powerful. Amid the media frenzy, the perspectives of those who face real challenges or offer critical insights can be all too often ignored or suppressed. This issue extends far beyond the silenced voices of supressed individuals or marginalized groups. It also encompasses a much broader concern for the non-human elements of our planet too. Those who, though not human, but play an essential role in sustaining human life. These crucial subjects such as the concerns relating to environment, ecosystems and animal species, often go unheard in the din of human-centric media, even though their existence directly impacts the future of humanity itself.

It needs to be emphasized that the challenges India faces are far from being local as they have significant global implications too. With 1.46 billion people, which is around 18% of the world's population, India plays a pivotal role in shaping and impacting global trends. Out of a global population of 8 billion, the actions and developments in India impact not just its own citizens but the entire planet. India's position as one of the fastest-growing markets, combined with its influence on key global issues like pollution, public health, standards of living and social behaviour, makes it crucial in determining the future of the world. Therefore what happens in India doesn't just affect its own people, but it resonates worldwide, impacting nearly one fifth of humanity.

It's important to recognize that India, as the cradle of one of the world's oldest civilizations with a profound religious and cultural heritage, brings an unique and invaluable perspective to global issues also. Any significant global challenge should, therefore consider the Indian context too. Indian ancient wisdom, philosophies and spiritual traditions offer valuable insights that can enrich contemporary discussions and solutions. India's deep-rooted values around interconnectedness, harmony with nature and collective responsibility can offer alternative frameworks that are often overlooked in mainstream global dialogue.

This book delves deeply into a range of pressing issues, both within India and the world, with a particular focus on amplifying the voices that are often silenced, those that carry pain, suffering and the weight of suppression. It seeks to shed light on the unheard or neglected narratives that are crucial to understanding the broader, often overlooked realities and to ensure these vital perspectives are given the attention they deserve.

Contents

KNOWLEDGE

When we start believing that we know a lot,
It is actually the time to understand how much more we still need to know.

1

HOW MUCH DO WE ACTUALLY KNOW?

OUR REFLECTION BRINGS to light the profound and humbling truth about our existence, how little we truly know about our origins, despite our vast advancements in knowledge. The more we seek answers to fundamental questions about life, the more we realize how much remains beyond our grasp. It's a striking paradox that in an age of unprecedented scientific progress, our understanding of our own beginnings still remains shrouded in mystery.

When we ponder the origins of life on Earth, we are confronted with an overwhelming ocean of unknowns. How did life begin? Was it the result of random chance, or is there some deeper force at work? What sparked the very first cell? (The basic building block of life as we know it) These questions have intrigued philosophers, scientists and thinkers for centuries and yet the true answers remain elusive.

And yet, amidst this important unknown, we often find ourselves fixated on issues that, in the real sense may seem insignificant. Our daily lives are often consumed with concerns that pale in comparison to the vastness of the universe and the unfathomable mysteries of existence. We argue over trivialities, engage in conflicts and chase fleeting desires, while the ultimate questions of life, our purpose, our origin, the reason for our existence remain largely unexplored.

This discrepancy between our focus on the immediate and our ignorance of the profound reflects a curious paradox of human nature. Perhaps, in our pursuit of understanding the small details of life, we lose sight of the bigger picture. Are we so engrossed in the noise of everyday existence that we forget to ask the essential questions? Shouldn't our desire to grasp the real story of how life began or to understand the real purpose of our existence be far greater than our concerns with the ephemeral matters of daily life?

Indeed, the very vastness of the universe serves as a humbling reminder of our insignificance. We are but fleeting moments in the cosmic timeline, mere specks in the infinite expanse of space. Yet, it is this very awareness that should drive us to seek deeper knowledge, to explore the mysteries of our existence with a sense of urgency and reverence. After all, how can we truly live without understanding where we came from, what we are here for and where we might be headed?

In this way, our thirst for knowledge, especially about our origins, should be a pursuit of the highest importance, not simply a passing curiosity. For understanding our origins, we gain a deeper appreciation of the extraordinary nature of life itself and perhaps even a clearer sense of purpose in the face of the vast unknown.

The origin of life and the formation of celestial bodies have been profound questions for humanity for millennia. Philosophers, scientists and theologians have long sought to understand when and how life began and how the universe itself came into existence.

The questions of when and how life originated and the creation of the Earth, Sun, Moon and stars are at the heart of some of the most enduring mysteries. The story of life's emergence, as well as the formation of our planet and the cosmos continues to evolve through scientific discovery that blends ancient curiosity with modern understanding.

One of the popular scientific version of creation of Earth is a fascinating tale that stretches across the vastness of time, a narrative spun from the depths of cosmic dust and the fire of distant stars. It is an exciting story written in the language of gravity, light and force, an ancient symphony that began possibly even long before the first spark of life flickered in the waters.

Science believe that in the beginning, there was nothing but an infinite sea of swirling gas and dust, elements that had been scattered by the death throes of long-gone stars. About 4.6 billion years ago in the quietest, darkest reaches of a galaxy, something stirred. Matter, drawn together by the invisible hand of gravity, began to clump, to collapse and to form something absolutely unique.

Like a master sculptor, gravity shaped this primordial mass into a spinning disk, with a fiery centre being the Sun and everything else slowly taking shape. Around this star, smaller particles collided and fused and from these cosmic dances, planets were born. Earth, like a newborn star, began as a molten ball, a chaotic whirlwind of fire and rock.

For millions of years, the planet was a world of constant volcanic eruptions, storms of dust and a sky ablaze with meteorites crashing into the surface. But, gradually, the Earth cooled. A thin crust formed, floating atop a roiling ocean of molten rock, while clouds began to gather above and rain fell, carving rivers and shaping valleys. In this quiet moment, the Earth began to soften, to heal.

The first oceans pooled in the deep basins and over time, they became the cradle for life, tiny, single-celled organisms that began the long, intricate dance of evolution. From the primordial soup, life began to grow, to diversify, to reach for the light in its many forms.

The Earth was not created in a single moment, but in a gradual unfolding, a long, slow process that continues to this day. It is a planet shaped by fire and water, by collision and erosion, by the steady pull of gravity and the delicate balance of forces. Earth is not finished; it is always in making and changing, just as we are.

From the smallest pebble to the highest mountain, from the deepest trench to the tallest tree, the Earth is a living, breathing masterpiece, constantly shaped by time and tide. A poem written in rock and water, in the winds and the stars.

With all these rich and diverse beliefs, it becomes not only important but essential to explore and understand the multitude of creation theories that have shaped human across cultures. These varying perspectives offer a profound tapestry of wisdom, guiding humanity's relationship with the world and our place within it.

With due respect to all other religious beliefs, it is pertinent to mention that the ancient Indian Hindu cosmology almost precisely matches with the scientific findings in regard to determining the age of the Earth, which is believed to be about 4.32 billion years (For more interesting details, one may find out more about the term 'kalpa' or one day of Brahma reckoned as 4,320 million years and considered to be the length of a single cycle of the cosmos).

In our pursuit of knowledge, we are called to appreciate that each belief reflects the unique historical, cultural and spiritual context of the people who have held it. But beyond mere respect for tradition, delving into these different views can enrich our own understanding of existence, offering fresh lenses through which to view life, the cosmos and the profound mysteries of creation.

What becomes clear is that while these narratives may differ in their details, they often converge in their recognition of the sacredness of life, the Earth and the profound interconnections between all beings. Whether one sees creation as a divine act, a cosmic accident or a process governed by natural laws, the questions that these beliefs address about the origins of life, the purpose of existence and the nature of the divine remain some of the most significant inquiries of the human existence.

By embracing these varied perspectives, we open ourselves to a deeper, more nuanced understanding of who we are, where we possibly come from and what our responsibilities are and with each other. The richness of these diverse world views allow us not only to seek answers but also to cultivate empathy, respect and shared wisdom in our common journey through life.

Knowing about all such views, whether religious, scientific or philosophical, invites us to move beyond rigid distinctions and to see the universal threads that bind us, offering a broader and more inclusive vision of our shared humanity.

The religious explanations of the formation of Earth and humans vary widely dissimilar across different faiths, each offering its own perspective on creation, the purpose of life and the relationship between humanity and the divine. However if we deeply try to understand these different theories and views, different languages of teachings and varied customs, which can be also be compared to different paths, but it seems to be leading to one destination, that is eternal peace and wellbeing of all.

NATURE

It is not only human voices that are suppressed,

Nature seems to be also in a greater pain.

2

IF NATURE COULD SPEAK

THE RELATIONSHIP BETWEEN nature, earth and human life is profound, intricate and inseparable. It is a relationship of interdependence, where every element, whether a blade of grass, a mountain peak or a human being, all plays a crucial role in the balance of existence. This co-relation is not just physical, but deeply spiritual, emotional and ecological.

Nature is the ultimate source of life. The Earth is a living entity, its ecosystems intricately woven together to create a world where life can flourish. From the air we breathe to the food we eat, the very essentials of human survival are gifts of nature. Plants and trees provide us with oxygen, the soil nourishes the crops that feed us and the water cycle keeps our freshwater supplies replenished. Every heartbeat of nature, every ocean tide, every seasonal shift, every life form is a reflection of the interwoven fabric that supports human existence. We know this, yet why do we often prefer to conveniently forget it?

But this connection goes beyond mere physical needs. Nature also provides the ecosystem that regulate climate, purify water, protect against floods and maintain biodiversity. The forests act as the Earth's lungs, while oceans regulate temperature and provide a wealth of marine life. Without nature's ability to maintain these systems, human life would be unsustainable. Simply, human life is a part of nature, not something separate from it.

The Earth is the canvas on which the story of life is beautifully painted, including humanity's own narrative. Our planet provides not only the physical environment for life to evolve but also the spiritual and cultural context that shapes human identity. We live on Earth, draw from its resources and dependent on it in countless ways. We should not consider Earth to be merely the surface beneath our feet, but rather it is the source of our existence, the place where we grow, live, suffer, cry and enjoy, We come to existence and perish, everything happens here.

The land, the water, the sky, all these elements are sacred because they represent life itself. Humans have evolved alongside Earth's systems, learning to adapt, thrive and sometimes even modify the environment to suit our needs. But in doing so, we must recognize that Earth is a living system and its health is directly linked to our health. If we degrade the soil, pollute the air or over consume the resources Earth provides, we jeopardize our own survival. In essence, harming Earth's ecosystems is a direct threat to the future of humanity and life.

Humans are part of nature, but our role has been complicated by our awareness, ingenuity and in some cases, our disregard for the Earth's limits. Unlike other creatures, we have the power to shape the environment, sometimes to our benefit, but often to our detriment. In our quest for development, advancement of technology and progress, we have often lost sight of our dependence on the Earth's natural resources.

Power always come immense responsibilities. As stewards of the planet, only humans have the capacity to harm or heal the Earth, to destroy or protect and restore the ecosystems and to understand the importance to live more harmoniously with the natural world. By recognizing the interconnectedness of all life - human and non-human. We can move toward a future where we act as responsible caretakers of the Earth, ensuring that its resources are sustained for future generations.

Human well-being is intrinsically tied to the health of the planet. Our physical, mental and emotional health depend on the ecosystems around us. Studies have shown that access to green spaces improves mental health, reduces stress and fosters a deeper sense of connection to the world. Nature provides us with more than just resources, it provides meaning, beauty and a sense of belonging. It is in nature that we find peace, clarity and inspiration - a reminder of the interconnectedness of all life.

Beyond the physical and ecological, there is a deep spiritual connection between humanity and the Earth. Many cultures and religions speak of the Earth as sacred, seeing nature not just as a collection of resources but as a living, breathing being with which we share a spiritual bond. Indigenous traditions, for example, view the Earth as a mother figure -Mother Earth, who nurtures all living beings. In this view, humans are not above nature but part of an intricate environment and therefore this sacred web of life demands respect, reverence and care.

Our spiritual well-being is often tied to this connection. The natural world offers a sense of wonder, awe and transcendence that reminds us of the larger mystery of existence. Whether through the stillness of a forest, the majesty of mountains or the vastness of the ocean, nature offers moments of clarity, renewal and understanding. It teaches us humility, patience and the importance of living in harmony with the world around us.

The co-relation between nature, Earth and human life is not one-sided. As human activity has grown more intensive, we have placed immense stress on the Earth's ecosystems. Climate change, deforestation, pollution and the loss of biodiversity are direct consequences of our inactions. These environmental crises are not distant threats, they are unfolding right now, affecting everything from food security to public health to the stability of global economies.

The destruction of ecosystems, whether through habitat loss, overfishing or the poisoning of water systems, it undermines the very processes that sustain life on Earth. The extinction of species disrupts the balance of ecosystems, leading to cascading effects that ultimately impact humans. Rising temperatures and extreme weather patterns threaten agriculture, displacement and the safety of entire communities. If we continue on this path of environmental degradation, the natural systems, we depend on will unravel and life, in all its forms, will face immense challenges in near future.

The relationship between nature, Earth and human life is a reminder that we are all part of the same, delicate ecosystem. The survival of humanity depends on the health of the Earth and the health of the Earth depends on the actions we take. We must learn to respect the natural world, recognizing that our fate is intertwined with the fate of the ecosystems. Our survival is not assured by technology or innovation alone, but it is assured by our capacity to live in harmony with nature.

The Earth is a living system that needs to be cared for, not just for the benefit of other species, but for our own survival. When we protect nature, we protect ourselves. When we restore ecosystems, we restore our own future. The co-relation is simple: the Earth is our home, nature is our lifeblood and humanity is a soul, tasked with ensuring that both are preserved for generations to come.

The question is not whether nature and human life are connected, as they are inseparably linked. The real question is whether we, as a species, will recognize and honour that connection before it is too late?

The importance of nature and the urgent need to save Earth for the survival of life cannot be overstated. Nature is not merely a backdrop to human activity but the very foundation of all existence. It is the complex, interconnected system that sustains us, nourishes us and provides everything we need to survive - air to breathe, water to drink, food to eat and ecosystems to regulate the climate and purify the environment.

At its core, nature is life's lifeline. It operates in delicate balance, where each element , from the smallest microbe in the soil to the vast oceans and towering forests, all plays a role in the great symphony of life. Biodiversity - the diversity of species, ecosystems and genetic variation is the backbone of this balance. When species thrive, ecosystems flourish, when ecosystems are healthy, the conditions for all life are maintained. Our survival is intertwined with this web of life. We are not separate from nature but we are part of it.

But we must remember that nature is not invincible. Human activity has disrupted this delicate harmony. Deforestation, pollution, overconsumption and climate change are all strains on the systems. We are witnessing the rapid extinction of species, the warming of the planet and the degradation of ecosystems that once served as the lungs, heart and circulatory system of the Earth. These are not distant problems, they are problems that threaten our survival, as they directly impact the air we breathe, the water we drink, the food we grow and the climate we depend on.

The Earth is facing unprecedented challenges, but it is also resilient. Nature has the remarkable ability to heal and regenerate, if given the chance. However, this recovery is not automatic or guaranteed. The damage we have inflicted on the planet is not just an environmental issue, now it is a survival issue. If we do not act now to preserve and restore the health of our ecosystems, we risk the collapse of the very systems that sustain life on Earth.

Saving the Earth means recognizing that we are stewards of this planet, entrusted with its care for future generations. It means transitioning away from practices that harm the environment and embracing sustainability in all aspects of life. It means protecting forests, oceans and wildlife and restoring the damage we have already caused. It means shifting from a mindset of exploitation to one of harmony, understanding that the survival of human life is deeply connected to the well-being of the natural world.

But beyond the physical survival of species, there is a profound, spiritual connection to the Earth. Nature is a source of awe, inspiration and wisdom. It reminds us of our place in the grand story of existence, offering us solace, clarity and a sense of belonging. We are part of the Earth, not apart from it.

The survival of life on Earth depends on our ability to recognize that we are not conquerors of nature, but caretakers. We must live with the understanding that the Earth is a shared home, one that we must protect and nurture, not just for ourselves, but for all living beings that call it home. If we continue down the path of destruction, we threaten not only the planet but the very essence of life itself. Yet, if we embrace our role as stewards and act with urgency, we can heal the Earth and create a future where life thrives, where nature and humanity coexist in harmony.

The Earth's survival is our survival. To save nature is to save ourselves. The time to act is now, because the clock is ticking, waiting for none.

Meta AI

3

SPLASHING WATERS ARE UNSEEN TEARS

WATER, ONE OF the five fundamental elements in ancient Indian philosophy, holds a profound significance not only in the metaphysical understanding of existence but also in the very survival of life on Earth. In Hinduism, the sacred texts often speak of the eternal cycle of creation and dissolution, where everything emerges from the five elements – earth (Prithvi), water (Jala), fire (Agni), air (Vayu) and Space (Akasha) and ultimately it returns to them in a seamless cosmic phenomenon. Water, as a symbol of fluidity, sustenance and transformation, stands at the heart of this philosophical framework, connecting all forms of life to the earth and to each other.

The land-to-water ratio on Earth is a marvel in itself, for it is this delicate balance that supports the intricate web of life. Covering about 71% of the Earth's surface, oceans, seas, rivers, lakes and aquifers are not merely bodies of water; they are life-giving reservoirs, intricately woven into the fabric of existence. Water shapes the planet's climate, nourishes ecosystems and sustains human civilization. Without it, the earth would be barren and inhospitable.

Water is often seen as the sustainer of life in its purest form. Its presence in rivers and oceans, its ability to cleanse and purify, mirrors the eternal nature of life itself, constantly in motion, yet ever-present. Water flows through the land like time through the ages, it nourishes the soil, cultivates the crops and ultimately, returns to the oceans, much like the cycle of birth, life and death that governs the universe. Just as rivers flow endlessly toward the sea, life too follows its course, destined to dissolve back into the elements from which it emerged.

The oceans, the vastest of all water bodies, are both the origin and the end. From their depths emerge the conditions necessary for life and into them, all that has lived will eventually return. Philosophically, the ocean symbolizes the ultimate source of creation, encompassing all life and providing the foundation from which existence springs. In the Vedic tradition, water is revered as a source of spiritual purification, as in the ritual of bathing in sacred rivers, which symbolizes a return to purity and harmony with the cosmos.

Rivers, with their continuous flow, represent the passage of time. They are the lifeblood of civilizations and their role in shaping history cannot be overstated. From the Ganges in India to the Nile in Egypt, rivers have been central to the rise and fall of empires, providing sustenance, trade routes and fertile lands for agriculture. The continuity of water symbolizes the unbroken thread of life, constantly renewing itself, yet never ceasing. Just as the river remains, so too does the essence of life, flowing towards its inevitable reunion with the cosmic ocean.

In a world where the natural elements are increasingly under threat, it is important to reflect on the ancient wisdom that recognizes the sacredness of water. Its preservation is not just a necessity for survival, but a call to honour the interconnectedness of all life. As we strive to understand the fragility of nature, let us remember that in the language of the elements, water speaks to us of continuity, transformation and the eternal cycle of existence. We are born from it, live with it and ultimately return to it. In honouring water, we honour the very essence of life itself.

4

THE OCEAN'S HEARTBEAT IS SLOWING

THE VAST, MYSTERIOUS oceans have long been the cradle of life on Earth, teeming with an astounding array of creatures and ecosystems. These marine realms, symbolizing both the source and the ultimate end of all existence, are now facing an unprecedented crisis. Human activities, driven by the quest for progress and consumption, are taking a severe toll on marine life and the quality of water in our oceans and seas. The delicate balance that sustains life in these waters is being shattered by pollution, global warming, over-fishing and habitat destruction, creating a grave existential challenge for the creatures of the deep.

The oceans represent the infinite, the eternal flow of life. Yet, as we exploit this great source of life for short-term gains, we are eroding the very foundation that sustains us. The pollution of the seas, particularly the proliferation of plastics, oil spills and chemical runoff, speaks to the recklessness with which we, as a species, have severed our connection with the natural world. The waters, once pure and untainted, are now choked with pollutants, suffocating marine life and disrupting the delicate rhythms of the aquatic ecosystems. Fish, whales, turtles and countless other species are paying the price for this disruption, their lives intertwined with the fate of the oceans, like strands in a cosmic web that cannot be easily unravelled.

The impact of global warming on marine life is equally profound. Rising sea temperatures, a direct consequence of the Earth's warming climate, have led to the bleaching of coral reefs, the destruction of vital habitats and the alteration of migration patterns for many marine species. Coral reefs, often referred to as the "rainforests of the sea," are not just beautiful ecosystems but vital to the biodiversity of the oceans. They provide shelter, food and breeding grounds for a myriad of species. As these fragile structures are bleached and die, the very foundation of marine life is threatened, leaving the oceans barren and devoid of the vibrant diversity that once flourished.

Moreover, overfishing has become another dark stain on the fabric of marine life. The insatiable demand for seafood, driven by human consumption and greed, has pushed many fish species to the brink of extinction. The disruption of the food chain, caused by the depletion of fish populations, sends ripples throughout the entire marine ecosystem. What was once a harmonious relationship between species is now a delicate, unbalanced system, teetering on the edge of collapse.

However, amidst these grave challenges, there are glimmers of hope. Efforts to protect and conserve marine life have begun to gain momentum. Many nations and organizations are working to establish marine protected areas, where human activities are restricted to allow ecosystems to recover and thrive. The international community has rallied around initiatives such as the United Nations' Sustainable Development Goal 14, "Life Below Water," which aims to conserve and sustainably use the oceans, seas and marine resources for sustainable development. Grassroots movements have also emerged, promoting sustainable fishing practices, reducing plastic waste and advocating for policies that address climate change.

These efforts represent a call to return to balance, to recognize the interconnectedness of all life forms and to restore the sacred relationship between humanity and the natural world. The oceans, in their silent wisdom, remind us of the impermanence of all things. They have the power to heal and regenerate, but only if we acknowledge the need for stewardship and reverence.

In the end, the protection of marine life is not merely about saving species; it is about restoring harmony with the Earth's most profound element, water. For in the oceans, we find not only the source of life but the ultimate reflection of our own interconnectedness with the cosmos. To safeguard the oceans is to safeguard the soul of the Earth itself.

HC warns all 7 CETPs of closure

Court: Improve Functioning In Three Months

'Riverfront Phase II to add to problem'

RIVER SUTRA

Ganga struggling for survival: Experts

Lockdown does what decades of schemes couldn't: Clean Ganga

Haider Naqvi & Sudhir Kumar

KANPUR/VARANASI: The nationwide 21-day lockdown to combat the spread of the Covid-19 is doing what ambitious schemes could not do over the decades — cleaning the Ganga.

Since 1986, when the Ganga Action Plan was conceived, the Central government has pumped in about ₹5,000 crore to clean a river considered holy by millions of Indians, but with little impact.

Now, real-time data from the Central Pollution Control Board (CPCB) shows that the water

5

RIVERS IN PERIL

WATER, THE LIFEBLOOD of Earth, has been a symbol of purity, sustenance and renewal in cultures across the world. Yet, in recent decades, the rivers that once nourished civilizations are now under grave threat. Water pollution, driven by industrial activities, urbanization, agricultural runoff and even to some extent religious practices, has transformed these once-pristine rivers into carriers of toxins and disease.

Many of the world's most vital rivers are facing severe ecological threats due to pollution, over-extraction, climate change and industrial development. For instance, the Yangtze River in China, which supports over 400 million people, suffers from heavy pollution and habitat loss, with over 70% of its freshwater species now endangered. The Ganges in India, sacred to millions, is among the most polluted rivers globally, with over 3 billion litres of untreated sewage entering it daily. The Nile, crucial for Egypt and surrounding nations, is under pressure from damming and water scarcity, while the Amazon, often called the "lungs of the planet" is being impacted by deforestation and mining runoff. Alarmingly, a 2021 UN report warned that nearly half of the world's large river systems are heavily fragmented, threatening freshwater biodiversity and the livelihoods of billions. These concerns highlight an urgent need for global cooperation and consensus in preserving the lifelines of our planet.

The Ganga, India's most revered river, holds not just geographical importance but spiritual and cultural significance too. It is considered the mother of all rivers, respected as Goddess Ganga in Hindu tradition. For millions, its waters are sacred, believed to cleanse the soul and wash away sins. Pilgrims flock to its banks for centuries, especially during the Kumbh Mela, seeking spiritual renewal and purification. The Ganga has sustained civilization for thousands of years, providing water for drinking, agriculture and transportation. Yet, this holy river, which symbolizes life, has become one of the most polluted rivers in the world, raising critical concerns about the interplay between human activity, spiritual reverence and ecological responsibility.

Historically, the Ganga's waters were pure and life-giving, supporting an abundance of flora and fauna. However, over the centuries, industrialization, urbanization, and population growth have put immense pressure on this river. The major sources of pollution include untreated sewage, industrial effluents, agricultural runoff and unplanned management. Cities such as Varanasi, Kanpur and Kolkata, which sit along the Ganga, discharge millions of litters of untreated sewage directly into the holy river daily. Industries along its banks release harmful chemicals, including heavy metals and toxic effluents, further deteriorating the water quality.

There have been concerted efforts to clean the Ganga. One of the most dedicated individuals in this cause was Dr. Guru Das Agarwal, an environmental engineer and former professor, whose life became synonymous with the battle to save the holy river. Dr. Agarwal, who later became known as Swami Gyan Swaroop Sanand, embarked on a crusade to protect the Ganga, advocating for the reduction of industrial pollution and the prevention of deforestation in its catchment areas. He emphasized the importance of reverence for the river and called for a comprehensive national effort to treat sewage and industrial effluents. Dr. Agarwal's dedication to this cause led him to fast for several months in 2018, ultimately sacrificing his life to highlight the urgent need for action. This was also an end of the hope of millions of people in India, who were silently waiting for some miracle to happen. Possibly, Dr. Agarwal was so much dedicated and focussed in his mission that he missed out on realizing the political and social transformation and changes in India from the times of Gandhi's 21 days fasts of 1943 to more recent era of Anna Hazare's fasting protest of 2003. Perhaps in today's times, only fasting for a good cause is not sufficient, one needs strong and efficient media management affordability, PR teams, event managers and modern day publicity techniques.

Despite the tireless work of scientists and activists, the river Ganga still remains heavily polluted. Why does this sacred river continue to suffer, even after so much has been invested in its cleanup? There are several reasons. First, India's rapid population growth, coupled with the lack of infrastructure in many regions, has led to an overwhelming burden on the river. The government's "Namami Gange" initiative, launched in 2014, aimed at cleaning the Ganga, includes measures such as constructing sewage treatment plants, controlling industrial effluents and creating awareness about waste management. While some progress may have been made, these efforts have allegedly been hampered by insufficient funding or local mismanagements, ineffective implementation and lack of public participation. Unfortunately, the political and economic factors driving industrial growth often take precedence over environmental concerns.

Moreover, the scale of the problem is so vast that the solutions proposed so far have only addressed the symptoms rather than the root causes of pollution. The unregulated discharge of untreated sewage and industrial waste continues unabated in many parts of the river. Many of the cities along the Ganga still lack adequate sewage treatment facilities and much of the river's water is used for irrigation, leaving little room for natural regeneration. Without a significant overhaul of wastewater treatment infrastructure, continued urban expansion and better enforcement of environmental regulations, true restoration of the holy Ganga may remain an elusive dream.

The plight of the Ganga is not an isolated issue. India is home to many rivers too, such as the Yamuna, Godavari and Narmada, that face similar challenges. These rivers, once the lifeblood of entire regions, are drying up, shrinking or becoming toxic due to uncaring human interference. The nearly 8% of the world's population that resides in India depends on these rivers for drinking water, food and livelihood. Yet, the rivers' survival is increasingly in jeopardy and with it, the fate of millions of people who rely on them.

The state of the Ganga and by extension, all of India's rivers reveals a deeper, more profound disconnect between humanity and nature. Rivers, in their most elemental form, symbolize the flow of life, of creation and destruction, of balance and harmony. The pollution of these rivers represents humanity's failure to honour this sacred connection. The river is not merely a resource to be exploited, rather it is a life-giving force that must be respected, protected and cared for. Just as the holy river Ganga is revered as a goddess, so too should the natural world be treated with reverence, its purity and vitality are the foundation of our own existence.

To address this crisis, a multi-faceted approach is needed. One that blends scientific innovation, serious governmental action and mass awareness and cultural change. The construction of more effective sewage treatment plants, stricter industrial regulations and better waste management practices are all essential. But equally important is a shift in consciousness, where the sacredness of rivers is once again recognized and upheld. Only when we acknowledge that the river is not just a resource but a living entity, integral to the ecological and spiritual balance of the Earth, can we begin to heal the damage we have inflicted.

Saving the Ganga and the other rivers of India is not just an environmental issue but a profound moral and philosophical challenge. It is a call to recognize that the fate of the river is inseparable from the fate of humanity. Only by restoring the river's health can we hope to restore our own. It is not just a concern for a huge population of India but it is also a concern for survival of around 8% world population too. Just because the rivers can't speak for themselves, we should not so conveniently suppress their painful voices.

Just like the pebbles, once jagged and distinct, are now eroded by the ceaseless journey with the flowing rivers, losing their sharp edges, their individuality, the course of society too seems to have drifted far from its origins. Like the ancient steps of the ghats, now eroded and weary from countless tides, time has worn away the essence of what once grounded us. The sacred truths, the tenderness of emotion, the shared humanity that once formed the foundation of our collective spirit have been slowly dissolved in the currents of material pursuit.

In their place, a hollow edifice stands tall, built on self-interest, veiled in the illusion of progress. Perhaps we have bartered inner light for outward shine, empathy for ego and reverence for convenience. The soul of society, once vibrant with compassion and spiritual awareness, now seems to echo the silence of forgotten values. And yet, perhaps in that silence lies the invitation, to return. To rediscover what the river could not carry away - the eternal within us.

6

THE EARTH BLEEDS GREEN

FORESTS, THE ANCIENT guardians of Earth are vanishing in silence, their voices lost in the roar of chainsaws and the blaze of unchecked fires. These great green cathedrals, once sacred to indigenous wisdom and revered by poets and prophets alike, are now seen merely as commodities, cleared in the name of progress, replaced by concrete, business profit and convenience. Rapid urbanisation has carved deep wounds into the lungs of our planet and with every tree that falls, a part of our collective breath falters.

The Amazon, often called the Earth's heartbeat, now beats with uncertainty, facing record-breaking deforestation fuelled by agriculture and illegal logging. Indonesia's rainforests are similarly being stripped for palm oil, displacing not just trees but entire species. Africa's Congo Basin, rich in biodiversity and cultural heritage is under threat from mining and development, while even the boreal forests of Canada and Siberia are not spared, burning each year with increasing ferocity as climate patterns spiral out of balance.

But who is truly responsible? Not just those who wield the axes, but also those who remain indifferent. Every product we consume, every decision made in ignorance, feeds this quiet apocalypse. The disappearance of forests is not just the loss of trees but it is the unravelling of ecosystems, the extinction of ancient lifeforms, the vanishing of ancestral wisdom and a betrayal of future generations.

If we continue on this path, can we truly hope to preserve the delicate balance of our planet? The time to act is not tomorrow, but right now. We need more than awareness, we need reverence, responsibility and a global consciousness that sees forests not as resources, but as sacred beings. The planet does not need saving as much as we actually need it. And to save ourselves, we must first learn to live in harmony with the roots that once sustained us.

7

CAN THERE BE A VOICE FOR THE VOICELESS?

ANIMALS DO NOT speak our language. They do not write their grief in books, nor do they protest in the streets or plead their cases in courtrooms. And yet, their suffering is as real as ours, often more so, because it remains unheard, overlooked and tragically normalized.

From the whimpering of street dogs abandoned to harsh urban conditions, to the anguished cries of elephants in circuses or the silent despair of animals in laboratories, the world continues to bear witness to cruelty inflicted on creatures who share this Earth with us. The tragedy lies not just in their pain, but in our indifference.

Philosophers across ages have pondered the moral duty of humankind toward animals. As Leo Tolstoy once wrote, *"As long as there are slaughterhouses, there will be battlefields."* Indeed, the way we treat the most vulnerable among us reveals the true nature of our collective soul. In a world driven by consumption and convenience, animals have been reduced to mere commodities, their intrinsic worth obscured by profit margins and cultural apathy.

Yet, through the fog of ignorance, there have always been radiant hearts who chose compassion over complacency. Among them, the name **Ratan Tata** stands tall. Known not only for his business acumen but also for his immense love for animals, Tata has dedicated a large part of his personal resources to animal welfare, particularly in providing shelter and medical care to stray dogs in Mumbai and beyond. He has quietly funded several animal care initiatives, believing that compassion towards animals is a reflection of a healthy and evolved society.

Maneka Gandhi, a long-standing advocate for animal rights in India, has spent decades bringing legal and societal reform to the treatment of animals. Founder of *People for Animals*, India's one of the largest animal welfare organization, she has worked tirelessly to introduce stricter laws, raise public awareness and promote cruelty-free living. Her belief that the dignity of life extends beyond humans has inspired many to re-examine their daily choices.

Recently, **Anant Ambani** has joined this esteemed league of compassionate icons. With the upcoming *Vantara Project*, an ambitious wildlife rehabilitation and rescue initiative, junior Ambani is setting a powerful precedent. The project aims to rescue, treat and care for injured, abused or abandoned animals, both domestic and wild, using advanced veterinary care and a deep-rooted philosophy of respect for all life forms. While the project has drawn attention for its scale and funding, its true significance lies in the message it sends: that the lives of animals matter and that kindness can be institutionalized at a grand level.

Across the world, countless others, known and unknown, have taken a stand. In Kenya, the *David Sheldrick Wildlife Trust* rescues orphaned elephants, giving them a second chance at life. In the United States, *The Humane Society* continues to fight factory farming and animal abuse through advocacy and education. Every region has its unsung heroes, rescue workers, shelter volunteers, vets and ordinary citizens, who respond to suffering with action, but lot more is still required.

Yet, the global scale of animal cruelty remains alarming. According to the World Animal Protection report, over 70 billion animals are farmed annually for food, with a vast majority subjected to intense confinement and brutal conditions. In laboratories, animals continue to be used for testing cosmetics, chemicals, and pharmaceuticals, despite the availability of humane alternatives. Wildlife trafficking, poaching, habitat destruction and entertainment-based exploitation (such as dolphin shows, circuses and roadside zoos) further add to the weight of this injustice.

The human-animal relationship is at a turning point. Are we to remain the tyrants of the natural world, or can we evolve into friends and guardians? The teachings of many indigenous cultures emphasize a deep spiritual bond with animals, seeing them not as property, but as fellow souls. Hinduism, Buddhism, Jainism and many other faiths echo similar sentiments that all life is sacred and that *ahimsa* (non-violence) is the highest form of virtue.

In today's digital age, every gesture, no matter how small it may be, resonates far beyond our screens. A shared post exposing cruelty or a single image capturing love between human and animal, or a compassionate comment can ripple through minds and awaken dormant empathy. Social media, though fleeting in nature, holds the power to plant enduring seeds of awareness. In a world often numbed by speed and distraction, even the simplest act of digital kindness can stir conscience and inspire changes. We must remember, the echo of our compassion, however subtle, can become the voice for those who cannot speak for themselves.

The time has come to listen, not just with our ears, but with our hearts. The silence of animals is not their consent. It is a test of our morality. If we, the so-called most intelligent species, cannot extend empathy to those who depend on us entirely, then our intelligence is hollow and our progress, deeply flawed.

Change often begins in small ways, everyday choices, adopting instead of shopping for pets, avoiding products tested on animals, supporting cruelty-free brands and spreading awareness. More importantly, it begins with the realization that animals are not "lesser beings", they also feel joy, fear, pain and love, just as much as we do. The only difference is that we have the power to choose how we treat them.

PEOPLE

Will the Suppressed Ever Be Heard?

8

A HISTORY OF SUPPRESSED VOICES

THROUGHOUT HISTORY, THE voices of the weak, the marginalised and the vulnerable have too often been drowned in the thundering loudness of powerful empires, or simply silenced by the weight of power and buried deep beneath systems built to sustain inequality. From the slave plantations of the American South to the colonised nations of Africa and Asia, from the persecution of indigenous tribes in America to the systemic oppression of lower castes in South Asia, the story of human civilisation is as much a tale of progress as it is of silence imposed on the powerless.

The pyramids of Egypt, the Taj Mahal of India, the Great Wall of China and the wealth of colonial Europe stand tall, but behind them lie the painful cries of countless unnamed labourers, slaves and victims whose struggles have rarely found space in history books. Their stories were never written, their suffering never acknowledged and their resistance either erased or vilified. The silence is not accidental, it is engineered. History, after all, has too often been written by the victors.

The transatlantic slave trade, which continued for over 400 years, forcibly displaced an estimated 12 million Africans. Their voices, stripped of language and homeland, still cry through time. Indigenous populations across the America were decimated not only by conquest but by centuries of cultural erasure. In India, the caste system institutionalised the marginalisation of millions, denying them basic dignity, education and opportunities. In modern times, racial injustice, gender discrimination, refugee crises and the plight of the working poor all echo this same ancient pattern - power overwhelming truth, might silencing morality.

Philosophically, this pattern points to a deep flaw in human nature, our tendency to dehumanise the "other" in order to justify dominance. As long as we view some lives as less valuable, some voices as less worthy, we perpetuate the cycle of injustice. Yet, history also teaches that silence can never last forever. The suppressed voices do rise, sometimes as whispers, sometimes as roars.

The Civil Rights Movement in the U.S., the anti-apartheid struggle in South Africa, women's suffrage and more recently, the global movements for indigenous rights, LGBTQ+ equality and climate justice, all bear witness to the resilience of the oppressed. These are not just political events, they are moral awakenings. As Martin Luther King Jr. said, *"The arc of the moral universe is long, but it bends toward justice."* But it only bends when enough people push against the weight of silence.

In the digital age, the tools of suppression have evolved, but so have the tools of resistance. Social media gives a platform to voices once confined to the shadows. Yet, we must remain vigilant. Tokenism, performative activism and misinformation threaten the purity of true justice. The challenge is not just to hear the silenced but to listen deeply, to understand, to feel with humility and act with courage and responsibility.

The question remains, Will we finally create a world where no voice is too small to matter? The answer lies not in power, but in conscience. And have courage to stand not with the loudest, but with the least heard.

Even the Suppressed has a Voice

9

IF I RAISE MY HAND, WILL YOU LISTEN?

THE HAUNTING IMAGE of a crushed small hand, smashed by the slabs of concrete scattered all around, emerging from the rubble of shattered and devastated house after a catastrophe, a tragic aftermath of an earthquake or a war lingers in the mind like a dark poem. It is a fleeting, yet profound reminder of lives once full of dreams, stories and songs, now buried beneath the weight of destruction. In that still moment, the hand, outstretched though motionless, seems to speak volumes - a silent testament to what was lost.

One can almost imagine the lives that once thrived beneath the wreckage, the child who might have been writing poetry in the quiet solitude of his home or perhaps singing a song that captured the beauty of a fleeting moment. What were his thoughts, his dreams, his joys before his world was suddenly torn apart? Before the earth cracked open or bombs fell from the angry sky or the storm consumed all in its wake? In the sudden and irreversible violence of such a catastrophe, such innocent lives were swept away in an haste, like notes in a melody that vanished before they could even reach their final chord.

The agonizing irony is that these lives, which once pulsed with meaning and potential, are now reduced to mere suppressed whispers, buried beneath the weight of rubble and ruin. The poetry of their existence, its tender verses, its fragile beauty is lost, suppressed forever by the unfair forces of nature or arrogant human cruelty. The songs that might have once brightened their hearts and enriched their days are silenced, not just for a moment, but for ever.

And yet, in the very image of that hand grasping at nothing, reaching out from the suffocating darkness, there is an echo. It is, as if the remains of these hidden lives still cry out from beneath the surface, their silent agony speaking through the debris. Perhaps it is not just their bodies that are lost, but the stories they held, the voices they shared with the world, their fleeting expressions of beauty and joy that were obliterated in the blink of an eye. We are left to wonder what words of wisdom, what laughter, what love was extinguished in that unfortunate moment.

In the midst of such devastation, we must ask ourselves, What does it mean for a life to be extinguished so suddenly, so violently? What is the cost of forgetting the faces behind the debris, of silencing the voices that once created something beautiful? Perhaps it is a reminder for us all to value the moments we have, to recognize the fragility of life and to honour the memory of those whose songs were cut short. Their stories live on in the space between the silence, in the hands that still reach out, in the hearts that continue to feel the weight of what was lost.

And though their voices may have been suppressed by the cruel hand of fate, we are called to carry their painful memories forward, to speak for the voiceless and to remember that, even in the rubble, there remains a deep and enduring voice of humanity that can never be permanently suppressed.

10

THE SUFFERING OF TRAFFICKED CHILDREN

IS THERE ANYTHING more cruel than taking a life? At first glance, one might say no. But delve deeper into the recesses of human cruelty and you'll find a fate that lingers longer and bleeds more slowly, being forced to live in agony that kills the soul, day by day. Killing is final, it is an end. But what about those who are kept alive only to be broken, piece by piece, in body, mind and spirit?

This is the silent torment of millions of children, trafficked, enslaved, exploited. They are not only robbed of their childhoods but also of their right to exist with dignity. They suffer in the shadows of a world that claims to be civilized, and it prefers to turn its face away from its darkest corners when voices of pain comes from its hidden hell.

According to the United Nations Office on Drugs and Crime (UNODC), nearly 30% of all detected trafficking victims globally are children. Girls are trafficked primarily for sexual exploitation, while boys are forced into labour, begging or armed conflict. Refugees and impoverished families, often desperate to survive, become the easiest prey. In India alone, over

47,000 children were reported missing in 2022, and a staggering 71% of them were girls.

These are not just numbers. Behind each statistic is a name, a face, a stolen future and a painful story. These are children whose laughter was silenced too early, whose eyes no longer reflect wonder but only fear, whose bodies bear invisible scars from a world that chose to ignore them.

Trafficking is a shameful form of commerce, profitable business of despair. Children are turned into merchandise and their innocence becomes the currency of organized greed. They are bought, sold, used, discarded, often with less compassion than a broken material object.

If death is the extinguishing of a flame, trafficking is a slow smothering of that fire. The victims remain alive, but only in the biological sense. Their identities dissolve. Their freedom is stripped. Hope becomes a forgotten word.

What could be more torturous than a life, where one can neither live nor die? A child forced to beg in filth, day after day, for someone else's profit, who is beaten for not earning enough! What remains of their spirit? A girl trafficked into prostitution, abused by dozens of men before she even understands what consent means, what remains of her soul?

This is not just cruelty; it is a path to social destruction. The torment is so deep, so prolonged, that death would seem a release. Yet they live, because their suffering is profitable for someone.

The tragedy is not just in the crime, but in the silence that follows it too. The comfortable world, safe, well-fed and entertained, often chooses not to see all these. It is easier to scroll past than to stop and care. The voices of these children are too faint to pierce through the noise of luxury, politics and vanity. Their cries dissolve into the background hum of the privileged.

We live in a time when the world can map the stars and build cities in the sea, yet cannot protect the most vulnerable among us. Why? Because protecting them demands not just laws and policies but it demands empathy. It demands that we not only look, but feel. Not only acknowledge, but act. And that is certainly no expected soon.

What does it say about us, that we have allowed such atrocities to thrive beneath our very feet? Philosophers have long argued that the essence of being human is rooted in our capacity for compassion, for moral responsibility. If we fail to respond to the suffering of trafficked children, we are not merely passive observers but we are complicit in their pain.

We must ask ourselves, What is the value of progress, if it cannot protect a child from being sold like cattle? What is the meaning of success in a world where millions of children cry to sleep in cages of abuse?

The stories of these children must not remain untold. Their pain must not be lost to forgetfulness. If more of the world knew and truly knew about the horror that unfolds in alleyways, brothels and basements, perhaps our collective conscience would stir.

We need voices louder than apathy. We need systems stronger to protect the week, we need hearts that has emotions and eyes that becomes wet, when others are so deeply wounded.

11

A PLEA FOR HUMANITY

THERE IS NO wound deeper, no silence heavier, than the cry of the innocent who suffer in the face of brutality. Across continents and centuries, the world has witnessed unspeakable acts of cruelty inflicted upon those who neither provoked nor deserved it, even children torn from their parents, lives ended before they began and communities shattered in the name of hatred, power or blind prejudice.

History remembers these moments not as tales of valour or triumph, but as shameful blots on the conscience of humanity. Atrocities against innocent and ordinary people, regardless of race, religion, nationality or gender, do not just damage the victims and their families but they scar the very idea of civilization. They question the moral fabric upon which nations claim to be built.

Whether it is a school shooting in Texas or a bomb blast in a mosque in Peshawar, the pain of losing a child is universal. A mother's cry in Gaza is no different from the anguish of a father in Uvalde or a grandmother mourning her grandchild in Kabul. Blood knows no nationality. Tears have no religion.

The Rwandan genocide of 1994, where nearly 800,000 people were killed within 100 days, remains one of the most horrific reminders of how quickly hatred can consume entire societies. The Holocaust, which led to the murder of six million Jews and millions of others by the Nazi regime, was not just an act of political insanity but it was a moral collapse that shook the very foundation of what it means to be human.

In history, certain moments stand as stark reminders of humanity's capacity for cruelty. One such moment, engraved in the collective memory of India and the world, is the Jallianwala Bagh massacre, an atrocity that reverberated through time, leaving an indelible scar on the human soul. On the fateful day of April 13, 1919, the British colonial forces, under the command of General Reginald Dyer, opened fire on a peaceful gathering of unarmed civilians, resulting in the death of hundreds, though the exact number remains disputed. Women, children, elderly, ordinary people, each with a story, a family, a life, became mere targets in a senseless display of power and ruthlessness.

The garden, once a place of solace, transformed into a memorial of shattered lives. The cries of men, women and children, caught between the rain of bullets and the high walls that confined their escape, still echo silently in the place, long after the sound of the firing ceased. These are not just the cries of physical agony but the cries of humanity itself, of justice trampled underfoot and of innocence lost in the shadow of imperial arrogance.

In the years that have passed, as time weaves its tapestry of progress, the memory of such events often fades. History becomes a distant echo and the pain of those who suffered is relegated to dusty pages in textbooks. But the Jallianwala Bagh massacre, like an ancient wound that refuses to heal, will never be forgotten. It is a stark reminder that the bloodshed of the innocent, once spilled, leaves behind more than just the physical remains, it leaves behind a legacy of pain.

Jallianwala Bagh represents the dark side of humanity's journey, a moment where civilization faltered and humanity was stripped of its compassion. It serves as a warning against the dangers of unchecked power, the dehumanization that can arise from oppression and the devastating impact of ignoring the cries of the innocent. The massacre is not just a page in history but it is a mirror to our conscience, urging us to reflect on our own actions, even today to safeguard the dignity of life and to ensure that such atrocities are never repeated.

Though the bullets have long fallen silent, the cries of Jallianwala Bagh continue to reverberate through the corridors of time, reminding us that the most brutal atrocities are not those that are committed in open warfare, but those that are inflicted upon the defenceless in the name of control, arrogance and dominance.

And even today, our collective failure to learn from history leads to repeating its darkest chapters. The cries of Kashmiri Pandits, who were driven out of their ancestral land in the 1990s amid terror and brutal killings, still echo across the valley. The pain of Nirbhaya, who was brutally gang-raped and murdered in the capital city of the world's largest democracy, triggered a national awakening, but the shadow of violence against women still looms large.

Can a civilized society ever justify burning two innocent children alive with their father as witnessed in Orissa, regardless of disagreement with the parents' beliefs? Imagine their cries, their mother's lifelong agony and the unbearable silence that followed. Such horrors not only scar families, they stain a nation's soul and shatter its image in the eyes of the world.

The recent murder of three men just for representing a particular religion or wearing a particular type of attire in a train, allegedly by an uniformed personnel deputed for ensuring safety of passengers, shattered our illusion of security in public spaces. The tragic death of Ankita Bhandari in the serene hills of Uttarakhand exposed the rot of entitlement, power and patriarchy. And the heart-wrenching fate of a little girl in a Kashmiri village, who only went out to graze her sheep and never returned, when her body was finally found, it stabbed the very soul of our society.

At the core of every atrocity lies a dangerous cocktail of dehumanization and indifference. When people are seen not as individuals but as labels - Hindu, Muslim, Jew, Black, White, Dalit, rich, poor, immigrant, it becomes easier to justify violence against them. Hatred needs an "other" to thrive. But what is most terrifying is not just the hate but the silence of those who watch it unfold.

Evil does not succeed because of the strength of the wicked, but because of the silence of the righteous.

Imagine the helplessness of a child watching their parents beheaded in front of them. Imagine the psychological scars of babies born in refugee camps, who have never seen their homeland and have only known hunger, fear and exile. How can we expect such children to grow up "normal"? Trauma becomes a legacy. Violence begets violence. And unless we interrupt this cycle with compassion, healing and justice, we are setting the stage for another generation of suffering.

It is a paradox that while humanity has reached the moon, decoded the genome and connected the world with technology, we still allow barbarism to exist in our neighbourhoods. We proudly talk of artificial intelligence while ignoring the real intelligence that lies in empathy. We celebrate freedom, yet millions live in dreadful fear.

No nation is immune. No ideology is exempt. The only defence against such horrors is a universal humanism that transcends all boundaries, a belief that every innocent life matters, that no child should pay the price for adult conflicts and that no woman should suffer because society failed her.

History must be remembered, not repeated, justice must be swift and fair, media and society must amplify the right and sensible voices, obnoxious voices must be ignored, governments must protect the vulnerable and most importantly there should be global unity against all kinds of atrocities

We have been hearing it so often, the ancient Indian scriptures describe the world as "*Vasudhaiva Kutumbakam*", *the world is one family*. But do we truly believe that? Because in a real family, the pain of one is the pain of all. A child crying in Gaza or in a school in Colorado should disturb our peace, not just make a passing headline.

In the holy Bhagavad Gita, Sri Krishna focused on '*karma'(a person's actions and deeds)*, therefore not birth, defines a person. Yet, society clings to the illusion of division, by caste, creed and religion, blind to the eternal truth that virtue transcends identity. If actions are the true measure of a soul, why do we revere labels over identities? The holy scripture offers not just spiritual guidance, but a profound antidote to societal hatred. But are we awakened enough to embrace this wisdom? Or do we, entranced by fleeting divisive politics and ego-bound identities, forsake the timeless call to see unity in diversity, and the divine in every being?

The Holy Quran emphasizes respect and tolerance toward other religions. It teaches that faith is a personal matter and that there should be no compulsion in religion (Surah Al-Baqarah 2:256). Allah says, *"To you be your religion, and to me mine"* (Surah Al-Kafirun 109:6), promoting peaceful coexistence with respect (Surah Al-Imran 3:64). Such verses encourage mutual understanding, dialogue and harmony among diverse faiths, reflecting Islam's message of peace and universal brotherhood.

Sikhism, as taught in the Guru Granth Sahib, emphasizes peace, equality, and universal brotherhood. Guru Nanak Dev Ji proclaimed, *"There is no Hindu, there is no Muslim....,"* affirming the oneness of humanity. The teachings promote living in harmony, serving others selflessly (seva) and seeing the divine in all. The verse *"Naam japo, kirat karo, vand chhako"* encourages remembrance of God, honest living and sharing with others, fostering unity and compassion. Sikhism rejects discrimination and upholds justice, urging followers to stand for truth and harmony. These principles form the foundation of a peaceful and inclusive world.

The Holy Bible teaches love, respect and kindness toward all, especially our neighbours. Jesus said, *"Love your neighbour as yourself"* (Mark 12:31), highlighting it as one of the greatest commandments. The Bible encourages compassion, forgiveness and understanding, regardless of differences. In Luke 10:27-37, the parable of the Good Samaritan beautifully illustrates that a true neighbour is one who shows mercy and care. These teachings inspire believers to build communities rooted in love, peace, and mutual respect, reflecting God's love for all humanity.

It is indeed paradoxical that while the core of every religion radiates peace, compassion and coexistence, these very faiths are often misused to justify hatred and violence. The sacred teachings, meant to unite hearts and elevate humanity, are frequently fragmented and manipulated to serve divisive agendas. Selective interpretations, stripped of context, become tools in the hands of those who seek power through discord. Tragically, many remain unaware, not only of other faiths, but of the true spirit of their own also, making them vulnerable to ignorance-fuelled propaganda. True enlightenment lies not just in ritual, but in reflection, empathy, and the courage to question. Until we awaken our minds to wisdom and open our hearts to understanding, such distortion will continue to fracture societies. Only through sincere dialogue, education and inner awakening can we reclaim the essence of religion as a force of unity, not division.

As long as the cries of the innocent are heard only in news clips and not in our hearts, humanity remains incomplete.

If we could listen closely to the echoes of history, we would hear the same message repeated across time and geography:

'Please, stop. Let no more children cry the way we did. Let no more mothers lose their sons to hatred. Let no more women walk in fear. Let there be peace, not in speeches but in streets. Not just in prayers but in reality.

Let the stories of those who suffered not be buried in silence. Let them be the reason we rise. Let them remind us, again and again, that *the highest religion is humanity and the greatest revolution is compassion.*

Meta AI

12

WHO IS RESPONSIBLE FOR AVOIDABLE ACCIDENTS?

ACCIDENTS ARE A tragic and inevitable part of human existence. Every day, lives are lost in ways that leave behind unspeakable pain and suffering. Some accidents occur beyond human control, like earthquakes, natural disasters and sudden calamities that defy prediction. But there is another category of tragedy, one that cuts deeper, one that strikes not because of fate, but due to human negligence, recklessness and mismanagement. These are the accidents where lives are lost not because of nature's fury, but because of human failure. And it is in these tragedies that the pain is more profound, not just because of the loss of innocent lives, but because we, as a society, fail to learn, to correct and to prevent.

The world has witnessed countless tragedies that echo through the annals of history. The Bhopal Gas Tragedy of 1984, where thousands of innocent people were killed in their sleep due to the negligence of a multinational corporation, serves as a haunting reminder of how corporate mismanagement and a lack of accountability can have catastrophic consequences. The Hillsborough Disaster in 1989, where 96 people lost their lives in a stampede during a football match, was a tragic reminder of how poor crowd management and disregard for safety protocols can lead to unimaginable loss. And who can forget the devastating Titanic disaster of 1912, where over 1,500 people drowned due to a combination of human error and arrogance.

But perhaps the most heart-wrenching of all are the accidents that happen on a daily basis in our streets, on our roads, in our trains and in our crowded public spaces. Road accidents, often caused by speeding, drunk driving or distracted driving, continue to take the lives of innocent pedestrians, children and families. Stampedes, fuelled by poor crowd management and lack of proper planning, have left hundreds dead in places of worship, festivals and other gatherings. All of these incidents share a tragic common thread, they could have been prevented.

Each life lost in these accidents is precious. Each person was someone's son, daughter, mother or father. Yet, despite the frequency of these tragedies, we seem to have become desensitized to the pain of these lives lost. The headlines may fade, the investigations may stall but the families of the victims are always left to mourn their losses in silence. But in their silence, there is a cry, a silent cry not for vengeance, but for justice. Not for punishment, but for change. These innocent lives do not demand retribution, they only demand that we, as a society should wake up.

Imagine the countless souls who have lost their lives in these tragic events. Their last moments were filled with terror, confusion and pain. Their loved ones were left in shock, devastated by the sudden loss, wondering why such an avoidable tragedy had to occur. And as the world moves on, these families are left behind, holding on to memories of lives that should never have been lost.

It is easy to become numb to these tragedies when they happen far away, when they are not directly connected to us. But every life lost, regardless of where or how, has an impact on the collective conscience of society. We, as a global community, must ask ourselves, What kind of world are we creating if we continue to tolerate preventable deaths at the hands of human negligence? How long will we continue to accept that innocent lives are lost simply because of poor decision-making, laziness or apathy?

The real tragedy lies not just in the accidents themselves, but in the lack of accountability that often follows. How many times have we seen promises made by authorities, organizations and corporations after such disasters, only for those promises to go unfulfilled? How many times have we witnessed investigations that lead to nothing, with no meaningful change to prevent similar tragedies in the future? The lives lost in these accidents cry out for justice, not in the form of compensation or punishment for the guilty, but in the form of meaningful reform and prevention.

We, as a society, must demand better. We must demand that our leaders and our institutions take safety and accountability more seriously. We must insist that they invest in infrastructure, training and planning to prevent accidents before they occur. We must ensure that the voices of the victims and their families are heard, not just in the wake of tragedy, but long before the next life is lost.

The innocent lives that have been lost in accidents caused by human error are not just numbers on a page. They are faces, They are names, They are the sons, daughters and parents whose futures were stolen from them because we, as a society, failed to take action on time. Their cries do not echo for retribution, but for prevention. They ask us to wake up, to listen and to take responsibility for the safety of every individual, everywhere possible.

The pain of loss is not just limited to the immediate family, but it ripples through communities and in the case of large-scale tragedies, through entire nations. These accidents should shake our collective senses of security and remind us that no one is invincible, that our lives are fragile and that it is our duty to protect them.

As individuals, we must be more aware of the choices we often make, whether it's our speed on the road, the way we treat others in crowded spaces or the importance of safety protocols in our work and leisure activities.

The cries of the innocent do not fade with time. They linger in our hearts, in our minds and in our collective conscience. And they call us to act. Every life lost in these preventable tragedies is a reminder that we are all responsible for the safety and well-being of those around us. It is not enough to just mourn for these lost lives. We must work responsibly to ensure that no more lives are lost in the same senseless, avoidable tragedies. Only then can we say that their deaths were not in vain.

Meta AI

13

THE RESILIENCE OF INDIAN MIDDLE CLASS

IN THE HEART of India's bustling cities and quiet towns, beyond the glitter of wealth and the anguish of poverty, exists a vast section of society that carries the burden of hope and hardship in equal measure - the middle-class and lower middle-class. They are not the loudest voices, nor the most visible faces in policy debates or media narratives, but they are the ones who keep the soul of the nation alive through their everyday struggle, silent sacrifices and unwavering resolve.

This class is not defined merely by numbers or income brackets. It is defined by dignity without privilege, sacrifice without applause and survival without support. These are people who neither beg nor expect Favors. They live with a quiet pride, one that prevents them from stretching their hands for help, yet compels them to stretch their limits for their survival. In a world that often measures success by extravagance, the middle class measures it by stability, self-respect and sustenance.

They dream, of a better home, of higher education for their children, of a holiday that doesn't need budgeting, of an illness that doesn't lead to bankruptcy. But these dreams are often distant stars, admired from afar, known to exist but never truly touched. Rising costs of living, stagnating incomes, sudden medical emergencies, job losses and unplanned family expenses strike them like bolts of lightning, abrupt, merciless and deeply unsettling. What for many is an inconvenience, for them becomes a crisis.

Their pain is not political enough to be debated on prime time, not dramatic enough to spark outrage and not impoverished enough to qualify for aid. Their voices are not suppressed by a system but they are silenced by life itself. They suffer not because they are weak, but because they are expected to endure. Society assumes their resilience and in doing so, forgets their vulnerability.

Every day is a new negotiation with rent, with school fees, with fuel prices, with medical bills and with their own sense of self-worth. And yet, they manage to smile. Not out of joy, but out of duty. They wear a mask of contentment so their children can dream a little more freely. Their superficial smiles conceal oceans of stress and their daily commutes become meditative journeys of silent prayers.

Their life is the truest embodiment of *karma yoga*, work done not for glory or gain, but out of responsibility and love. They are the quiet monks of modern society, sacrificing comfort for continuity, luxuries for life and peace for perseverance. Their stories may not be written in books, but they are etched in every electricity bill paid late, every school uniform stitched with care, every postponed vacation and every cup of tea shared at the end of an exhausting day.

No government scheme, no economic policy and no social movement can be truly complete unless it acknowledges the quiet desperation of this class. They don't need pity, they need policies. They don't seek charity, they seek fairness. Above all, they deserve to be heard, not as numbers on a statistical chart, but as individuals whose contributions and challenges shape the nation in silent but steadfast ways.

14

THE UNHEARD VOICES OF THE TAXPAYERS

IN EVERY NATION, there exists a quiet majority, the taxpayers, who, without much recognition, form the economic backbone of their countries. They rise early, work long hours and contribute a significant portion of their hard-earned income to the state in the form of taxes, believing that this collective contribution will return to society in the form of better infrastructure, healthcare, education and social security. But increasingly, around the world and more so in nations like India, these contributors find themselves asking - *Is anyone listening?*

Taxpayers around the globe expect fairness, transparency and accountability from their governments. Their expectations are simple and justified - judicious use of public funds, quality public services, equitable development and a governance model that respects their sacrifices. However, in many countries, developing and developed alike, those expectations are frequently met with disillusionment. Scandals of corruption, reckless public spending, misallocation of resources and visible disparities between tax collection and the quality of public services fuel a growing sentiment of betrayal among the people who fund the system.

In the United States, the debate over fair taxation is ongoing, with the wealthiest 1% controlling over 30% of the country's wealth while benefiting from legal loopholes to minimize their tax liability. In the UK and several EU nations, austerity measures have often targeted public services while corporate giants continue to benefit from favourable tax regimes. The disparity between the expectations of taxpayers and the delivery of services is not just economic but it's deeply emotional and moral issue.

In India, the dynamics are more complicated. Out of a population exceeding 1.4 billion, only around 7 crore individuals (approximately 5%) file income tax returns, and just around 2% of the population actually pays income tax. This minority shoulders the financial weight and burden of running a nation of immense scale, diversity and needs.

Huge portion of these income tax-payers belong to the salaried class, individuals with fixed incomes, limited deductions and minimal scope to "manage" their tax liabilities. For them, every increment in tax rate directly impacts their disposable income, often reducing their ability to save, invest or spend on their families' well-being including education and health requirements. Despite this, they continue to contribute, year after year, driven by a sense of civic duty and hope that their sacrifice will lead to national progress.

In contrast, business owners, large corporations and professionals often have the legal and structural means to minimize their tax liability. Through a complex web of exemptions, creative accounting and tax havens, a significant portion of potential tax revenue slips through these cracks. While not all tax-saving strategies are illegal, the ethical disparity is glaring.

The most painful truth for Indian taxpayers is that despite their regular contributions, the quality of public goods and services remains largely inadequate. Government hospitals are overcrowded and under-resourced. Government schools often lack teachers, facilities and basic infrastructure. Roads, especially in non-urban areas, are poorly maintained. Public transport, sanitation and water supply systems are either broken or substandard in many regions.

What do taxpayers want? Their expectations are neither grand nor unreasonable. Transparency in Governance, Accountability for Corruption, Improved Public Services, Equity in Taxation and Dignity and Recognition.

There is also an expectation of such *voices*. Most taxpayers in India do not belong to vote-bank politics or influential lobbies. Their pain, when expressed, is often dismissed or drowned out. As they remain politically underrepresented, they become the most convenient group to squeeze further when fiscal deficits rise.

Taxation is meant to be a noble act, citizens contributing toward the collective good. But when that contribution turns into compulsion, devoid of returns, the act loses its meaning. A society that fails to protect and acknowledge its most responsible members fosters quiet resentment and weakens the social contract.

There is a silent suffering that comes with being a responsible citizen in a dysfunctional system. The honest taxpayer is bound by duty but is offered little in return. They see grand statues erected, VIP convoys roaming in super luxury and government schemes announced with pomp, while their children are enrolled in overcrowded schools, their parents wait in government hospital corridors and their daily commutes become endurance tests.

The emotional toll is immense. It is not just about money, it is about fairness. It is about wanting to see a nation grow with your contributions.

The taxpayer is not just a source of revenue, they are a symbol of trust in the nation's promise. When that trust is broken repeatedly, it doesn't just erode the economy, it erodes the spirit of democracy. It is time we listened to the silent pillars of the society who support the financial stability of our nation.

15

FREEDOM OF EXPRESSION IN THE AGE OF ONLINE ABUSE

IN AN AGE where digital platforms promise unprecedented freedom of expression, a paradox emerges. Social media, meant to connect minds and voices across boundaries, often becomes an abusive battleground of harsh words, personal attacks and toxic intolerance. People from all walks of life, whether an acclaimed actor, a renowned writer, an outspoken activist or an ordinary user, anyone can face relentless trolling, harassment and abuse simply for sharing their views and opinions. What was once envisioned as a democratic space for dialogue has increasingly turned into a hostile environment, especially when the shared content touches upon sensitive social, political or religious issues.

The reality is stark. An innocent opinion, a piece of thoughtful writing or even a creative expression can trigger waves of online vitriol. The mob mentality that social media fosters fuelled by anonymity and numbers does not just disagree with a perspective but it seeks to silence it. This intolerance is not limited to controversial posts or offensive rhetoric but it extends even to well-meaning and constructive criticism, often misinterpreted or twisted out of context.

Famous personalities are particularly vulnerable, as their posts are instantly visible to millions. Many famous personalities has often been trolled for her their political views, despite consistently maintaining a rational and respectful tone. Author and Journalists also face not only verbal abuse but death threats and attempts at character assassination, simply for holding the powerful accountable or simply asking tough questions. Even global figures such as Malala Yousafzai, whose advocacy for girls' education won her a Nobel Peace Prize, have been subjected to online abuse, reflecting the deeply rooted discomfort many have with strong, vocal individuals, especially women.

The problem runs deeper than personal attacks; it reflects a larger cultural issue. As thousands jump in to abuse someone for their views, it signals a worrying trend of intellectual suppression. The ancient philosopher Socrates once said, *"Strong minds discuss ideas, average minds discuss events, weak minds discuss people."* Unfortunately, the trend on social media today often seems to glorify the latter, with little space left for nuanced debate or intellectual exchange.

Every abusive remark, personal attack or trolling of those with differing views reveals a deeper emptiness, a bankruptcy of ideas, logic or substance. When one lacks reason or merit to defend their stance, frustration often finds expression to insult. But truth stands firm on facts and reason, it needs no rage to assert itself. A mind rooted in understanding debates, it does not demean. Thus, hostility in discourse is not a sign of strength, but of weakness, a loud confession that one's argument cannot withstand the quiet strength of reasoned thought.

This culture of intolerance erodes the very foundation of a healthy society. If thinkers, writers, teachers and artists begin to fear expressing themselves, the society loses its moral compass. It loses the capacity to reflect, to question, to evolve. Silence becomes a defence mechanism for many, especially those with self-respect and dignity. They retreat from public discourse, wary of the backlash, the insults, the vile threats. What remains is an echo chamber where only the loudest, most aggressive voices dominate, shaping public opinion in dangerous directions.

Moreover, when abuse replaces argument, it reflects more on the abuser than the abused. As Friedrich Nietzsche once observed, *"Whoever fights monsters should see to it that in the process he does not become a monster."* The inability to engage with differing opinions respectfully is a form of intellectual immaturity, one that poisons public discourse and stunts societal progress.

There is an urgent need to restore civility and empathy to online spaces. Disagreement is a natural and necessary part of any democracy, but it must be expressed through dialogue, not derision. We may not agree with every post or perspective, but we have the choice to respond thoughtfully, or simply scroll past. Abuse is not expression, it is a form of suppression, a signal that diversity of thought is under siege.

To preserve the democratic spirit of social media, users must embrace responsibility along with freedom. Platforms too must play a more active role in curbing hate speech and protecting users who are vulnerable to targeted harassment. But most importantly, as individuals, we must re-learn the value of listening, the grace of silence in disagreement, and the courage to speak kindly even when we dissent.

In a world increasingly divided by digital screens and ideological bubbles, it is only through mutual respect and tolerance that we can hope to create a society where every voice, famous or ordinary, agreeable or challenging, can be heard without fear. For the health of our public discourse, the dignity of our thinkers and the future of our nation, we must reject the culture of abuse and reclaim the lost art of peaceful and constructive conversation.

Cyber Crime
Victims
Meta AI

16

ONLINE FRAUD IN INDIA: A GROWING THREAT

THE DIGITAL REVOLUTION in India has brought immense opportunities, but it has also opened the floodgates to a worrying surge in cyber fraud. With over 800 million internet users and more than 1.2 billion mobile connections, India stands as one of the largest digital ecosystems in the world. Yet, this rapid digital penetration, combined with socio-economic vulnerabilities and gaps in cyber security enforcement, has made the country a soft target for online fraud.

According to the National Crime Records Bureau (NCRB), cybercrime cases in India have grown significantly in recent years. In 2022, more than 65,000 cybercrime cases were registered, a sharp increase of around 24%. The NCRB report of 2024 suggest reporting of fraud losses exceeding Rs.33,165 crores in last four years, including Rs.22,812 crores in 2024 alone. However, cybercrime experts believe the actual number of incidents could be several times higher, as many cases go unreported due to lack of awareness or fear of social stigma.

Among the most common types of online frauds are phishing calls, UPI frauds, investment scams, fake KYC alerts and deceptive messages about electricity disconnection or expired insurance policies. Fraudsters impersonate bank officials, government employees or law enforcement agencies, often using fear tactics to pressure victims into sharing OTPs, card details or making immediate payments.

Senior citizens are among the worst affected. Having grown up in a more trusting environment, many are ill-equipped to recognize modern digital threats. With limited digital literacy, they often fall prey to scams involving pension disbursements, health insurance or fake legal threats including the latest scams of 'digital arrests'.

The youth, especially unemployed graduates and laid-off IT professionals, also face dual threats, being victims as well as being lured into becoming part of fraudulent operations, either knowingly or unknowingly. The alarming unemployment and job-loss rate, has left many skilled individuals vulnerable to manipulation, often getting recruited into cybercrime networks under false pretences.

What's even more alarming is the growing role of international syndicates. Recent investigations have exposed cybercrime rackets operating from foreign countries such as Cambodia, China and Nigeria, targeting Indian citizens using spoofed numbers and cloned websites. India's large English-speaking population and vast digital banking network make it an attractive target.

According to a 2023 report by the Indian Cyber Crime Coordination Centre (I4C) under the Ministry of Home Affairs, there were multiple instances of international criminals collaborating with domestic cyber gangs. In several big cases, huge amounts were siphoned off through fraudulent investment apps mimicking legitimate platforms etc.

While telecom operators and banks have started broadcasting warning messages, such as the now-familiar "never share your OTP or bank details", the reach and effectiveness of these alerts remain limited. These warnings, though well-intentioned, often go unnoticed or are treated as routine background noise by users.

There have been notable steps to increase awareness. Initiatives like the 'Cyber Dost' Twitter handle by the Ministry of Home Affairs, Digital Literacy campaigns, and the 1930 National Cybercrime Helpline have improved first-level reporting mechanisms. Financial institutions have also ramped up customer education, SMS alerts and real-time transaction monitoring.

However, the investigation and prosecution side remains weak. The conviction rate in cybercrime cases is abysmally low, only around 2% as per NCRB data. Many state police forces are under-equipped and under trained to handle complex, cross-border digital crimes. Cybercrime cells often lack forensic capabilities and inter-agency coordination remains a challenge.

Mainstream news often misses the human side of these frauds. The devastated voices of senior citizens who lose their life savings or middle-class families whose education funds vanish overnight rarely receive adequate media attention. The trauma faced by these individuals is both emotional and financial, often resulting in long-term psychological distress. Our media often ignores such incidents as small value individual cases, failing to realize the awareness value of such news having impact on millions of ordinary people.

17

CELEBRATING THE VISIONARIES - INDIA'S BUSINESS LEADERS

IT IS NOT a crime to be rich. In fact, wealth, when earned through innovation, perseverance, and ethical practices, becomes a powerful tool for nation-building. Unfortunately, in recent times, a disturbing narrative has taken root in public discourse, one that unfairly paints all wealthy individuals with the same brush, often labelling them as exploiters or "Dhanna Seths" in an attempt to win over the lesser privileged masses. This misplaced rhetoric not only undermines the spirit of entrepreneurship but also diminishes the transformative contributions of many business leaders who have played pivotal roles in shaping modern India.

A shining example that rises above this noise is Sir. Ratan Tata, a name that inspires reverence across the globe. Humble, visionary and deeply compassionate, Ratan Tata's legacy extends far beyond balance sheets and market shares. Under his mentorship, the Tata Group not only grew into a global conglomerate but also emerged as a beacon of ethical business and corporate social responsibility. From health care to education, rural development to disaster relief, the Tata Trusts have touched millions of lives, often silently, without seeking applause. His refusal to chase personal wealth in favour of public good is a testament to what true respectable leadership looks like.

Sir. Ratan Tata is not alone. India is fortunate to have a league of entrepreneurs and industrialists whose contributions have helped propel the country towards progress. Anand Mahindra, Chairman of the Mahindra Group, is known not just for business acumen but for his vision of inclusive growth. Through initiatives in affordable mobility, rural development, and skill-building, he has consistently pushed the envelope of what responsible capitalism can achieve. His social media engagement reflects not only his intellect but his humane approach to leadership.

Adi Godrej, the architect behind the Godrej Group's expansion into diverse sectors, has been a strong advocate of sustainable development and corporate governance. His commitment to environmental and social sustainability continues to set benchmarks in Indian industry.

Then there's Azim Premji, often referred to as the "czar of Indian IT," who transformed Wipro into a global software giant. More importantly, through the Azim Premji Foundation, he has committed billions of dollars towards improving education in India, focusing especially on underprivileged communities. His philanthropy, often understated, is among the largest in the world and a proud reflection of Indian generosity and conscience.

In the new age of startups and digital disruption, India's youth have found new idols, visionaries who turned bold ideas into powerful movements. Vijay Shekhar Sharma, the founder of Paytm, is one such icon. Hailing from modest beginnings, Sharma's innovation brought about a digital payment revolution in India. Paytm empowered millions, including small vendors and rural communities, by giving them access to cashless transactions and digital banking, long before it became mainstream. The company's role in India's financial inclusion story is not just significant but it is historic.

India's thriving startup ecosystem has given rise to a new generation of business leaders whose ambition is matched by their sense of purpose. Ananya Birla, part of the new-age Birla legacy, is not just an entrepreneur but a changemaker. With ventures in micro finance and mental health awareness, she represents a blend of business acumen and social responsibility.

Food delivery was never the same after Deepinder Goyal and Pankaj Chaddah introduced Zomato. Starting as a simple restaurant directory, Zomato evolved into a global brand that revolutionized food tech, created thousands of jobs and reshaped consumer behaviour. In a similar vein, platforms like OYO, Swiggy, Nykaa and Freshworks have transformed the Indian business landscape, giving global corporations a run for their money.

As of 2023, India has produced over 100 unicorns, startups valued at over $1 billion, making it one of the fastest-growing hubs of innovation in the world. This explosive growth is not just a statistic, it is the result of tireless efforts by visionary young minds who dared to dream and took risks to solve real-world problems. They have created employment, contributed to GDP and helped India emerge as a global digital powerhouse.

The youth of India recognizes these efforts. Far from seeing wealth as a vice, they see it as a reward for innovation, a tool for empowerment and a pathway to self-reliance. Business leaders who create value, uplift communities and adhere to ethical standards are not to be vilified but to be celebrated.

At a time when global economies are struggling and job creation is a challenge, these entrepreneurs and industrialists have become revolutionary agents of change. They've instilled hope in a generation that now sees business not just as commerce, but as a calling.

The real essence of India's success story lies in this silent revolution, in factories and offices, in labs and cafés, in tech parks and rural startups, where dreams are built, not on entitlement, but on grit, vision and compassion.

To vilify wealth or success is to misunderstand its real purpose. Wealth, when guided by values, can heal, educate, employ and inspire. India needs more wealth creators, more Ratan Tatas, more Anand Mahindras, more Azim Premjis, more Ananya Birlas and Vijay Shekhar Sharmas, who dream not just for themselves, but for the growth of the nation. As a society, our role is not to stereotype or stigmatize, but to support and salute those who build, lead and serve.

Because in celebrating them, we also celebrate the brighter, bolder India they help shape every single day.

Meta AI

18

WHY SHOULD ANYONE BE STRANGERS IN THEIR OWN COUNTRY?

EVEN AFTER 75 years of India's independence, the dream of an united, inclusive and empathetic nation remains, in many ways, unfulfilled. The Constitution of India promises equality and dignity to every citizen, regardless of region, race or language. Yet, a painful irony persists, there are countless Indians, including from the Northeast and hilly regions who also serves our Indian army in huge numbers and brings pride any glory to the nation in sports, but continue to be treated indifferently at times.

Despite being an inseparable part of India, people from states like Manipur, Nagaland, Arunachal Pradesh, Mizoram, Meghalaya, Assam, Sikkim and Tripura often find themselves subjected to humiliation, racial slurs and exclusion when they travel or live outside their home states. In places that pride themselves on cosmopolitanism, like Delhi, Mumbai, Pune and Bengaluru, these citizens are often subjected to humiliation, treated with suspicion or made the targets of casual racism by some groups and individuals.

The Northeast is one of the most culturally vibrant and historically rich regions of India. Yet, its people are often judged not for who they are, but for how they look. Unfortunately individuals with East Asian features are frequently labelled as "foreigners" or "Chinese," even by those who consider themselves educated. They are mocked for their food, language, attire or accent. Such narrow-mindedness not only reflects a lack of awareness, but a deep-seated bias that goes unchallenged far too often.

It is unfortunate that while the warm-hearted people of the Northeast welcome visitors with grace and respect in their own states, they are often not met with the same kindness or respect when they travel to other parts of India. They often feel that true unity lies in mutual respect, not just in words, but in action and attitude.

In a 2014 study by the North East Support Centre & Helpline, it was reported that a huge percentage of people from the Northeast residing in Indian metros had experienced some form of racial discrimination. From being denied housing facilities to being harassed on the streets, their experiences paint a grim picture of a society still struggling to embrace its own diversity.

In cities like Bengaluru, considered a hub of global ideas and modern thinking, there have been multiple incidents where people from the Northeast have been assaulted, called racial slurs or denied access to basic services. The 2017 case of a Naga student in Bengaluru who was refused entry into a restaurant for "not looking Indian" is just one among many such shameful examples.

When violence or unrest occurs in the Northeast, it rarely garners the same national attention or empathy as similar events in other parts of India. This selective indifference deepens the alienation. The pain of Northeastern communities is often either misunderstood or completely overlooked by the mainstream narrative. Their issues become regional, not much national, an unfortunate division that further distances them from the collective Indian identity.

India, as a nation, was built on the foundations of unity in diversity, a phrase we often repeat, but seldom honour in spirit. The beauty of India lies in its pluralism, hundreds of languages, dozens of religions and an endless array of cultural traditions coexisting in one democratic framework. Yet, when we make people feel like strangers in their own country, we betray that very essence.

What does it mean to belong? Is it only about sharing a passport or should it be about shared respect and dignity? The moment one citizen feels alienated because of their appearance or origin, the soul of democracy suffers a deep painful wound.

The time has come to reflect deeply on the kind of nation we wish to be. A nation is not just a landmass or a collection of laws, it is a shared dream, a moral promise. Every citizen, regardless of where they are from or who they are, deserves to feel at home in any corner of their country. That is not just a constitutional right, it is a human right paramount to national interest.

Let us listen to the aggrieved voices. Let us walk beside those who have been made to feel small, different or unwelcome. And let us affirm, in our words and actions, that no Indian should ever feel like a stranger in their own land.

Food adulteration: A global public health concern

Dr Mahendra Pal* and Dr Meenu Mahinder**

₹1.5cr pepper coated with cancer-causing oil seized

Times News Network

Chennai: The food safety department on Wednesday seized 18 tonnes of adulterated pepper coated with cancer-causing mineral oils such as liquid paraffin and burnt diesel oil in Broadway.

A team of officials raided the godown of a wholesale dealer on Varadha Muthiappan Street and seized adulterated pepper worth ₹1.50 crore and 400 litres of mineral oil. "We sealed the godown of Venkateswara Traders and took

...substances causes more than 200 diseases – ranging from diarrhoea to cancers. •

The Great Indian Toxic Food Fraud

RTI response finds adulteration rate very hig

About 40% of food items adulterated

G JAGANNATH | DC
CHENNAI, SEPT. 26

About 40 per cent of food items tested by government labs in the state in 2013-14 were either adulterated or "misbranded", Food Safety and Standards Authority of India (FSSAI) statistics said.

Interestingly, the rate of adulteration in Tamil Nadu is two times higher than that of the national average of 19 per cent, according to information availed from FSSAI through RTI by this newspaper.

Food samples tested range from commonly used items such as edible oil, masala powder, dals, salt, sugar and grains to ready-to-eat packed foods available ed from the markets and tested to find whether it met the set standards or not.

The rate of adulteration found in food samples tested in the state has gone up by four times from 8.43 per cent in 2011-12 to 39.66 per cent in 2013-14.

A senior official of the food safety administration department attributed the high rate of adulteration or misbranded food items found in the state to lifting of more suspected samples from the market rather than taking random ones. "We mostly take food samples based on complaints from people, officials or media reports. That is why the rate of adulteration in the food samples tested in

used items are norma adulterated. In edible oi used cooked oil is mix with fresh oil. Pepper po der packets sold in the m rkets are mostly adulter ed with cornstarch wi only five per cent pepper said sources.

Consumer activist and under trustee of the Co umer Association of Ind R Desikan said that he w not surprised by the lar adulteration found in fo samples tested in the sta He said that traders, hote ers and manufacturers the state are making eve effort to prevent enfor ment of the FSSAI Act filing numerous cases ag nst it in various cour There are about 34 cas filed in various cou

MAJOR SUGGESTIONS BY LAW COMMISSION

A FOOD ITEM IS SAID TO BE ADULTERATED IF

1,000 KG ADULTERATED GHEE SEIZED FROM FIVE COTTAGE INDUSTRIES

DC CORRESPONDENT
CHENNAI, OCT 30

Over 1,000 kg of adulterated ghee was seized from five cottage industries in the city on Tuesday.

The food safety department acting on a tip-off raided five places on Shastri street and Bharathi Street in Kaveri Nagar, Saidapet, and found that several tins of ghee were ready to be sent to places for con-

"Another problem was that the packets were made to look like they were sent from a factory from elsewhere. Names like Erode, Thiruporur and Tiruppur, were found on packets," Kadhiravan said.

Around 1,000 kg of ghee were seized and samples were sent to the food lab for testing. Being perishable, most of the products will be destroyed in a day or two after documenting it, Kadhiravan

19

THE POISONED PLATE

IN A WORLD that boasts of technological advancement, medical breakthroughs and scientific marvels, a disturbing paradox continues to plague millions, the very essentials of life are being laced with poison. From fake medicines to adulterated baby food, from pesticide-laden vegetables to chemically ripened fruits, an insidious threat creeps silently through the kitchens and hospitals of countless homes, particularly in underdeveloped and developing nations of South East Asia, including India. It is a crisis that strikes not with guns or bombs, but with syringes, spoons and shopping bags.

This is not merely an issue of fraud, it is a moral betrayal of the deepest kind, a betrayal of trust, of life itself.

The problem is not new, nor is it limited to isolated incidents. It is systemic, pervasive and shockingly organized. In India alone, multiple high-profile crackdowns have exposed entire networks producing fake medicines, many of them indistinguishable from legitimate ones. Life-saving drugs, meant to fight cancer, heart disease or infections, are being counterfeited and sold in the open market, leaving the sick not only untreated but further endangered.

In 2023, the World Health Organization (WHO) allegedly flagged several Indian-manufactured syrups after they were linked to child deaths in countries like Gambia and Uzbekistan. The very medicines meant to protect the most vulnerable allegedly became the agents of death, a chilling reminder of how high the cost of negligence can be.

Then there are the countless unreported tragedies, especially in rural areas, where access to authentic medication is limited and awareness is low. The poor, who often have no choice but to rely on whatever medicine is available, become easy targets of this dark industry.

But the menace does not end with medicines.

Walk into any local vegetable market and beneath the vibrant colours and inviting aromas lies another hidden danger. Reports about artificial colouring agents, wax coatings, carbide chemicals and pesticides far exceeding safe limits being used on fruits and vegetables to enhance appearance and shelf life. What looks fresh and nutritious is often a cocktail of toxins.

Most disturbing, however, are the cases of adulterated baby food and synthetic milk, made from detergents, urea and even synthetic oils, materials that have no place in any food, let alone something consumed by infants and children. Several large-scale busts in India have revealed factories producing fake milk and ghee under the names of trusted brands. In these acts, we witness not just criminality, but an assault on innocence itself.

What is the emotional and philosophical cost of this silent, slow poisoning?

It is the agony of a mother who, despite her poverty, saves enough to buy medicine for her ailing child, only to find that it was fake. It is the quiet dread of a father feeding his family with vegetables he knows may be unsafe, but has no other option. It is the slow death of trust in a system meant to protect, not prey on, its own people.

These are not just health hazards. They are wounds on the soul of society.

What does it say about our civilization when we allow greed to poison milk meant for babies, or pills meant to heal the dying? When the ethics of profit overshadow the sanctity of life, we drift far from the ideals of any civilized society.

The tragedy deepens with the realization that while the crimes are organized, the response is not. Enforcement is sporadic, penalties are weak and convictions are rare. The regulatory bodies tasked with ensuring food and drug safety are allegedly underfunded, understaffed and often hamstrung by corruption.

Meanwhile, the average citizen has little recourse. With no way to verify the authenticity of what they consume, most are forced to rely on faith alone, faith that is often betrayed. The worst victims are the poor and uneducated, who not only suffer physically, but live under the constant burden of fear and helplessness.

This is more than a public health emergency, it is a system collapse, a deep moral crisis that questions the very foundation of our collective conscience.

Civilizations are judged not by the grandeur of their monuments or the strength of their economies, but by how they protect their most vulnerable. And by that measure, the widespread adulteration of food and medicine is a damning indictment.

Have we become a society where profit or politics justifies all acts? Where the hunger for wealth blinds us to suffering? Has the soul of business become so hollow that we no longer recognize the value of life?

We must ask ourselves- What is the worth of a society where food cannot be trusted and medicine cannot be relied upon? If our children cannot grow without fear, if the sick cannot heal without risk, what kind of future are we heading towards?

This crisis cannot be solved by legislation alone. Laws must be enforced, yes, but conscience must be awakened. A section of the business community must rise above short-term profits and uphold the integrity of their products. Government agencies must be empowered and made more accountable. Whistle blowers must be protected and encouraged. And most importantly, consumers must be informed, vigilant and united, with a more powerful voice.

We need a massive awareness campaign, not just in cities, but in every village and town, to educate people about food safety, medicine authentication and reporting mechanisms. Technology must be harnessed to build traceability and transparency into supply chains.

But above all, we need to reclaim our moral compass.

Let the milk we feed our children be pure not just in substance, but in intention. Let the medicines that promise healing never carry the shadow of death. Let our vegetables and fruits nourish not only the body, but our faith in humanity.

Only then can we say that we are truly progressing, not merely in GDP, but in reality.

"It is better 100 guilty Persons should escape than that one innocent Person should suffer."

Benjamin Franklin

Meta AI

20

A CRY FROM THE DARK CELLS

THE INJUSTICE OF Undertrial Detention is not a new concept. In the vast corridors of justice, where the rule of law is meant to uphold the dignity of every individual, a haunting silence echoes, the silence of those who wait behind bars, not as convicts, but as undertrials. They are not proven guilty. They have not been convicted by a court of law. Yet, their lives remain suspended in dark prison cells, trapped in a system that promises justice but delivers delay.

This is not just a flaw in the legal mechanism. It is a wound in the soul of any democratic nation that prides itself on the principles of fairness, liberty and human dignity.

According to the **National Crime Records Bureau (NCRB) 2022**, over **70% of India's prison population** are undertrials, people who are yet to be proven guilty. That means out of every 10 people in Indian jails, more than 7 have not been convicted by any court. They are in prison for no crime yet proven, often simply because they are poor, unrepresented or forgotten.

This situation is not merely a legal technicality, it is a humanitarian crisis. Many of these undertrials spend years, even decades, waiting for their trial to begin or conclude. In some shocking instances, individuals have been acquitted after 10, 15 or even 20 years, their innocence proven only after the prime of their lives was stolen behind iron bars.

It is often said that *"Justice delayed is justice denied,"* but in some of the case of prolonged undertrial detention, justice is not just denied, it is destroyed.

Imagine a young man arrested on suspicion, unable to afford legal aid, languishing in jail for a crime he didn't commit. By the time he is acquitted, he has missed his education, lost his family, been branded a criminal by society and lost his self-worth. The question arises: can any system, however just on paper, restore those years? Can it bring back lost youth, shattered dreams or the respect of a society that already judged too soon?

The philosopher Fyodor Dostoevsky once said, *"The degree of civilization in a society can be judged by entering its prisons."* If that is so, then the overburdened, under-resourced and deeply unjust reality of undertrial crisis paints a painful picture of our collective conscience.

There are many reasons behind this cruel paradox, case backlogs, shortage of judges, lack of legal aid, poverty, illiteracy and social prejudice. India has a judge-to-population ratio of 15 to 20 per million far below what is required for timely justice. The average Indian courtroom is burdened under thousands of pending cases and the wheels of justice move at a glacial pace.

While the Supreme Court of India and various High Courts have from time to time expressed deep concern over undertrial detentions, but this is not merely a bureaucratic or judicial issue. It is a reflection of how we, as a society, treat the poor, the voiceless and the marginalized. Most undertrials come from disadvantaged communities, Dalits, tribals, minorities and the economically weak. Their lives are weighed down not only by the charge against them but by the deep-rooted biases of society itself.

Moreover, the cost of this injustice is not only borne by individuals. It burdens the state, too. According to estimates, India spends over ₹6,000 crore annually on maintaining its prison population, money that could have gone into education, health or legal reforms.

The Indian Constitution guarantees the right to life and personal liberty under Article 21. Yet, every undertrial whose fate hangs in limbo is a grim reminder that these rights often exist more on paper than in practice.

Their stories do not make front-page headlines. Their faces are not seen on television debates. But their pain, their patience and their profound loss cry out for reform.

Let us remember, the measure of a just society is not how it treats the powerful, but how it safeguards the powerless.

India may have sent missions to the moon, pioneered digital payments and emerged as a global voice. But until we look into our prisons and listen to the unheard cries of the innocent behind bars, our progress remains hollow.

21

THE FORGOTTEN VOICES OF ADIVASIS

ADIVASIS, OR THE tribal communities of India, are not just another demographic, they are the *original inhabitants*, the soul of this ancient land. Their roots run deeper than kingdoms, deeper than empires; they are entwined with the rivers, forests and hills that have nurtured their way of life for thousands of years. Yet, in the name of civilisation, development and modern governance, these children of nature have long been pushed to the margins of society.

Historically, across the world, indigenous peoples have been the first to face the harshest consequences of colonisation and "progress." India is no different. With over 8.6% of the Indian population (which is over 10 crores) identified as Scheduled Tribes (according to the 2011 Census), the Adivasis represent a rich mosaic of languages, customs, spiritual beliefs and ways of living that are in harmonious dialogue with the environment. But the past few centuries and especially the last few decades, have not been kind to them.

Their forests have been taken for mining. Their lands have been cleared for industries. Their rivers have been dammed and their hills blasted. All too often, many of them feel that decisions about development have been made not *with* them, but *against* them. What not sufficiently explained or discussed but simply termed "national interest" frequently translates into displacement, cultural erosion and silence for the tribal voice.

Entire communities have been relocated in the name of infrastructure or resource extraction. In states like Chhattisgarh, Jharkhand, Odisha and parts of Maharashtra and Madhya Pradesh, the story repeats itself, tribal homes replaced with factories, their sacred groves replaced with smokestacks. The Forest Rights Act of 2006 was a step forward, acknowledging their connection with the land, but a section of them still feel that the implementation has remained inconsistent and even superficial.

Their concerns, over livelihoods, identity and autonomy are at times real and urgent. But when these voices are unheard for too long, frustration festers. In some regions, the turn to armed rebellion activities, which has been a tragic and more harmful for them. Many urban people and activists distanced themselves from their concerns even though they were sympathetic towards them for their losses. The rise of insurgent groups claiming to speak for tribal rights has, unfortunately, cast a long shadow over the very cause they claim to defend. Violence, while born out of despair, has distanced their struggle from empathy and given the state further justification to respond with force. The community also needs to understand that any revolution takes time, peaceful discussions can only get them desired results.

The truth is, the genuine concerns of tribal communities are neither violent nor unreasonable. They seek dignity, not dominance. They want education for their children, not erasure of their language. They ask for healthcare, not helicopters. They want their gods to remain in the forest temples and their customs to survive amidst changing times.

Historically, the Adivasi struggle is not against development, it is against the cost of development without justice. It asks a profound question: can a society truly call itself progressive if its first people are its last priority?

During the British rule, the Adivasi groups in India have suffered enormously due to the cruelty and rapid urbanisation plans of the then government without any sympathy or care towards them, however after independence also the expectations of the tribal people of India were not completely met, however in recent past the interest taken by both the PM Modi or LOP

Rahul Gandhi and other important leaders towards connecting with them raises a new hope for their developments. India in fact must listen, not just as a state, but as a civilisation. If we ignore the wisdom of those who have lived in harmony with nature for generations, we lose more than just their culture, then we lose a part of our collective soul.***

22

ANXIETIES OF A GENERATION

IN THE QUIET corridors of business-schools and the buzzing lecture halls of universities, in the minds of millions of young dreamers, there brews a growing storm, anxiety, uncertainty and a haunting question: *What does the future hold for us?*

Across the world, youth are grappling with a reality far removed from the promises they were once told. From New York to New Delhi, from Beijing to Berlin, the story is strikingly similar, the path forward is no longer as clear.

At the heart of this crisis is the rapid transformation brought by technology. Artificial Intelligence, robotics and automation are not just reshaping industries, but they are redefining the very idea of human labour. Jobs once done by people are now being performed more efficiently by machines. From basic customer service roles to complex analytical tasks, automation is replacing routine and in some cases, even creative work. The World Economic Forum's "Future of Jobs" report predicts that by 2025, over 85 million jobs globally could be displaced by automation, even as 97 million new roles emerge, many of which require advanced, specialized skills that current education systems are struggling to teach.

But technology is not the only storm cloud. The world is also grappling with trade wars, economic nationalism and strained geopolitics. International student mobility is no longer a guaranteed aspiration. Increasing visa restrictions and changes in policies, rising tuition fees, political distrust and tighter immigration policies have made it harder for youth from developing countries, especially India to easily access education and employment abroad. The dream of moving to America, Europe or Australia for a better future is slowly turning into a distant dream.

In India, the situation is more complex and more critical. The youth here are not just navigating global uncertainties but they are also battling deeply embedded domestic challenges. Over the years, job creation has not kept pace with the growing workforce. According to CMIE (Centre for Monitoring Indian Economy), India's unemployment rate touched nearly 8% in 2024, with youth unemployment far higher, especially among educated graduates.

The public sector, once the bedrock of stable employment, has shrunk visibly. Vacancies in government departments remain unfilled and recruitment drives have become infrequent and competitive beyond reason. Even when they occur, students often face another heartbreaking hurdle in form of paper leaks, corruption and nepotism. Several high-profile examination scandals from SSC to state-level exams have shattered faith in the fairness of the system. For a young aspirant who studied day and night, only to see the opportunity vanish in the hands of fraud, the emotional toll is devastating.

In the private sector too, job growth has slowed. Automation has reduced entry-level roles, while many employers demand experience from freshers who are yet to be given their first opportunity. Skill development remains a challenge. Many students graduate with degrees, but not with employable skills reflecting a deeper flaw in the education system and planning.

In such an odd situation, frustration is inevitable. Mental health concerns among youth are rising. Dreams are being postponed with uncertainty and in some tragic cases, abandoned altogether. Some turn bitter, others retreat into silence. But in every silent stare, every rejected application, every postponed exam, there is a story of immense pain that the society cannot afford to ignore.

A society is judged not just by how it treats its elders, but by how it nurtures its youth. The future does not belong to the rulers of today, it belongs to the young minds who must carry the nation forward. If the current generation of decision-makers continues to dismiss the worries of the youth as impatience or rebellion, they fail to see that they are alienating the very architects of tomorrow.

Senior citizens may hold the reins of power today, but the pulse of a nation beats in its young hearts. Their voices must be heard, their concerns must be addressed and their potential must be protected. The youth do not merely seek employment, they seek purpose, dignity and a chance to contribute meaningfully to their nation. And when these aspirations are ignored or denied, it is not just individual futures that are dimmed, but the collective destiny of the nation.

India, a nation that boasts of its demographic dividend, cannot allow that very dividend to become a burden. Policies must evolve not just to boost statistics, but to heal the despair. Education needs a renaissance, employment a revival and good governance a moral duty.

As a society, we must stop offering hollow motivational quotes to the youth and start building real bridges through transparency, fairness, investment in education, innovation in employment and above all, have empathy. Because when the youth falter, the future stumbles. And when they rise, the nation roars and soars.

23

THE UNHEARD CRIES OF THE IMPECUNIOUS

IN THE GREAT concert of human civilization, where nations sing songs of economic growth, innovation and power, there lies a silent undertone of a quiet, aching hum of pain, poverty, and despair. These are the unheard cries of the impecunious, the destitute, those who exist at the invisible margins of the world's progress. Their suffering is profound, yet their voices rarely find space in policy debates, headlines or national narratives.

Across the developing and underdeveloped nations of Asia and Africa, the statistics paint a grim reality. According to the World Bank, as of 2023, over 700 million people globally still live in extreme poverty, surviving on less than $2.15 per day. A significant portion of this population resides in South Asia and Sub-Saharan Africa, where income inequality, lack of access to healthcare, education and clean water and systemic neglect create an unending cycle of despair.

Even in economically rising nations like India, where GDP growth is indicating as a global success story, the contrast is painfully stark. Even in prosperous cities like Mumbai, Bengaluru, Delhi or Surat, one can witness two worlds coexisting, gleaming skyscrapers and luxury malls standing tall beside slums where people live in cramped tin-roofed shelters, where clean drinking water is a luxury and a one-time meal is not guaranteed. According to NITI Aayog's 2021 Multidimensional Poverty Index, a considerable percentage of people have escaped out of the poverty level but still a huge percentage of our population still remains in such extreme poverty levels, a number that, despite progress, reflects the harsh reality faced by millions.

The image of a child or an old man scouring a garbage bin for a morsel of food, or an old woman lying curled beneath a plastic sheet during a monsoon night or a labourer collapsing on a scorching street in a heatwave, is not a distant nightmare. It is the everyday truth for countless human beings. And yet, these lives remain hidden in plain sight often ignored not just by systems of power, but by society's conditioned and accepted indifference.

In a world governed by optics, where nations compete for global image and investment, the existence of extreme poverty becomes an uncomfortable truth. Media, often dictated by commercial interests and political narratives, rarely allows these real stories to surface. There is an unspoken censorship, not imposed by law, but by convenience. The presence of the poor is seen as a stain on the shining image of national success. And so, their suffering is filtered, erased or left unspoken.

But what kind of progress are we truly celebrating, if it comes at the cost of human dignity? What does it mean to rise as a nation while allowing millions to sleep hungry, unclothed and uncared for? Progress that silences the weak is not progress, it is merely consolation.

Poverty is not merely the absence of wealth, it is the absence of voice of recognition. It is a state where a person is not just deprived of food or shelter, but of being *seen* as human. And herein lies the gravest tragedy, not that poverty exists, but that we have normalized it. We have become immune to the suffering that does not touch our own skin.

In the deeper moral compass of humanity, this indifference is a wound to our collective conscience. Civilizations are not judged by their wealth or weapons, but by how they treat their weakest. The poor may not have a vote bank large enough to sway elections or the resources to make headlines, but they possess what is most fundamental, the right to live with dignity.

The climate crisis further deepens this divide. The poor suffer disproportionately from floods, heatwaves, diseases and displacement. They have the least carbon footprint, yet bear the greatest brunt of environmental destruction. In 2023, heatwaves in India claimed hundreds of lives, many of them daily-wage workers who could not afford to stay at home. During the monsoons, thousands in urban slums are displaced or fall ill due to waterborne diseases. The urban poor, particularly, live in some of the most vulnerable conditions imaginable with no safety nets and little public sympathy.

Solutions, of course, require policy intervention, more inclusive welfare, better public healthcare, investment in affordable housing, equitable education and safety nets that actually reach the poor. But beyond economics, what is needed is a social awakening, a culture of compassion. The first step is to see the poor not as burdens, but as fellow humans. Their struggle is not theirs alone, it is a mirror to the soul of society.

Let us not measure a nation's greatness by how high its towers rise, but also by how deeply its roots of compassion run. Let us build a world where no one needs to beg for food, search trash for survival or die anonymously in a city that never noticed their existence.

24

IF THE GREAT SOULS COULD SPEAK

IF THE SPIRITS of those who laid down their lives for India's independence could walk among us today, one wonders, what would they say? What would *Bhagat Singh*, who embraced the noose for his dream of a just and united India, feel seeing the country gripped by corruption, communal hatred and growing inequalities?

Perhaps *Mahatma Gandhi*, who preached non-violence and truth as the pillars of Swaraj, would sit silently, saddened by the noise of hate-filled rhetoric, by the manipulation of power, by the divisiveness that has crept into the soul of the nation. He may whisper through his silence: "*Did I fast so that the real purpose of independence may be ignored?*

Netaji Subhas Chandra Bose, who dreamed of an India free not only from foreign rule but also from mental slavery, would surely be pained to see how the fight for freedom has been replaced by a struggle for chairs, where service has turned into self-interest and sacrifice has faded into slogans. "*You gave me blood and I gave you freedom*," he might say. "*But what are you giving the future now? Hatred? Division? Corruption?*"

Even *Dr. B. R. Ambedkar*, the architect of our Constitution, who envisioned an India where justice, liberty and equality would not just remain ink on paper, would look upon the present with grave concern. The marginalised still suffer, the system still bends to privilege and the voice of the common citizen often drowns in a sea of power politics. He may well ask, "*Was my pen used only to write what would later be practically ignored?*"

The very essence of the freedom movement was unity across caste, creed and community. It was a movement powered by ethics, empathy and shared dreams. Yet today, we see that dream fractured by political propaganda, social polarization and institutional decay. The air is heavy with suspicion, debates have turned into diatribes and elections have become more about division than development.

If these heroes could speak, they would not shout, they would *plead.* Not for themselves, but for the soul of the nation. They would urge today's youth not to forget the price paid for freedom. They would remind us that the tricolour is not a symbol of any one ideology, but of every Indian's dignity and dream.

And if they stood at India Gate or beneath the shadow of a national flag fluttering against a polluted sky, they might simply say: *"You are free, but are you just? You are independent, but are you united? You have power, but where is the purpose?"*

History gave us freedom. The question now is, can we honour it? Or will we allow the blood that soaked the soil of independence to dry without meaning?